MARTIAL ART BASICS

thai boxing

MARTIAL ART BASICS

thai boxing

MARTIN FOLAN
5th Degree Black Belt

I would like to dedicate this publication to my mother and father and all my family, to my son Kieran, who is my life and inspiration, to my partner Angie, and to all my instructors, past and present.

PLEASE NOTE:

The author, packager and publisher cannot accept any responsibility for injury resulting from the practice of any of the principles and techniques set out in this book. If you are in any doubt about your level of health and fitness, please consult a medical professional before attempting any of the techniques.

Published in 2008 by Grange Books
an imprint of Grange Books Ltd
35 Riverside, Sir Thomas Longley Road,
Medway City Estate, Rochester,
Kent ME2 4DP
www.grangebooks.co.uk

British Library Cataloguing-in-Publication data available on request.

ISBN 978-1-84804-023-6

1 3 5 7 9 10 8 6 4 2

AN EDDISON•SADD EDITION
Edited, designed and produced by
Eddison Sadd Editions Limited
St Chad's House, 148 King's Cross Road
London WC1X 9DH
www.eddisonsadd.com

The text and illustrations in *Martial Art Basics: Thai Boxing* were previously published in card deck form as *Martial Art Basics: Muay Thai* in 2006 by Connections Book Publishing (UK), Barnes & Noble Books (US) and Gary Allen (Aus).

Phototypeset in Zurich using QuarkXPress on Apple Macintosh

Printed in Singapore

CONTENTS

INTRODUCTION

Why Thai Boxing?

Thai Boxing – also known as Muay Thai – is a very dynamic and powerful martial art that uses hands, feet, elbows and knees to overcome an opponent. Enjoyed around the world by people of all ages and abilities, Thai Boxing offers something for everyone, whether you want to:

- experience training in a martial art;
- improve general fitness and flexibility;
- gain confidence and boost well-being;
- learn a method of self-defence;
- compete in Thai Boxing as a sport.

In addition, students from other disciplines are now increasingly turning to Thai Boxing to supplement their own training. This is due to its wide-ranging physical benefits and extremely versatile striking techniques. With the huge rise in popularity of mixed martial arts competitions (such as the K-1 tournaments), more and more martial artists are incorporating Thai Boxing in their cross-training, and discovering the benefits for themselves.

This book is the perfect way to supplement your training, whether you are taking up Thai Boxing for the first time, are already an experienced practitioner, or are adding it to your own training system. All the basics are clearly presented step by step, with easy-to-follow instructions, and hints and tips are given throughout, to help you get the best results. The book is an ideal training aid, and can be used any time, anywhere. So off you go!

History and rituals

Thai Boxing is an ancient battlefield art of Thailand (formerly Siam). Its origin as a fighting style is thought to have developed over the centuries from Krabi Krabong, the martial art that formed the basis of the deadly fighting techniques used by Siamese warriors. Precisely how long Thai Boxing has been around, however, is unknown, as all official records were lost in the 1770s, when the Burmese laid siege to the Siam city of Ayuddhaya: the city was overrun, ransacked, and put to the torch, and all treasures, religious relics and works of art, as well as the royal archives, were destroyed. Thailand's history has since been pieced together mainly from European visitors and from Burmese, Cambodian and Chinese sources.

Thai Boxing is known as the 'Science of Eight Limbs', in reference to the weapons of the body used to defeat an opponent (hands, feet, elbows and knees). Traditional Thai Boxing fighters used to wear hemp (rope) on their hands, and were known to apply resin to the hemp and then dip their hands in broken glass – luckily, a custom that is no longer practised! Modern tournament fighting was introduced in the 1930s, with the introduction of weight categories – as found in Western boxing today.

Nai Khanom Tom

Many regard Nai Khanom Tom as the father of Thai Boxing. One of the Siam soldiers captured by the Burmese in the 1770s, he was given the opportunity to gain his freedom by fighting the greatest Burmese soldier. Upon defeating the soldier, he would then have to face another, and another, until he had fought twelve in total, overcoming them with his remarkable fighting techniques. He was then given back his freedom. A yearly tournament is held every March at the Lumpini Stadium, Bangkok, in honour of this great fighter's name.

Wai Kru

Dating back several centuries, and still performed to this day, the Wai Kru is the tradition of paying respect to your teacher(s), your parents and the things you hold sacred. It is a demonstration of respect and gratitude, and is carried out by kneeling down and placing your hands in the 'wai' (prayer) position, then leaning down and placing both hands on the ground, palms facing down. This is done a total of three times, to complete the Wai Kru.

Ram Muay

The Ram Muay (known as the 'boxer's dance') is a ritualistic and traditional dance unique to each Master, who will then teach it to his students (you will need to perform it as part of your grading). Although the content of the Ram Muay may differ from camp (club) to camp, the basic principle remains the same.

It consists of a variety of movements that generally includes sweeping the arms, balancing on one leg in a guard-like position while circling the knee, standing on the front leg and lifting the rear leg up and again performing sweeping movements, then a stamp into a squat-like position, putting both arms out to the side, and raising back onto one leg for the finish. It may sound rather odd – especially to those who don't practise martial arts – but it is a truly beautiful set of moves to behold.

In the modern Ram Muay, in competition Thai Boxing, the student will walk around the ring touching the top rope, approaching and touching the corner posts with a prayer, showing respect to his opponent and to the spirits. He may also stamp in the opponent's corner, to show his superiority (during which time the opponent will move away from his corner).

The club

For many with a newfound love for the martial arts, that first step through the door of a club (also known as a camp) can be a nerve-racking experience. Don't let it be. When you look around, you will see students of all levels, but don't be intimated; we all have to start at the beginning – you won't be the only one.

The *Kru* (instructor) should make you feel welcome from the moment you first arrive. They will introduce themselves, as should you, and will then ask how they can help you: what you wish to gain by training in Thai Boxing; whether you want to compete, train for fitness, or just wish to learn the art; whether you would like to progress in the grading system. Any good club will not push you into anything, but only encourage you in what you personally want to achieve from learning Thai Boxing. The students at the club will be there for a whole host of reasons, whether they are training to stay fit, wish to become fighters (or are already fighters), or simply wish to take part in a club activity.

Remember: you do not have to become a fighter. This is entirely a matter of personal choice. Although a fair number of Thai Boxing practitioners do end up competing, if you don't wish to fight you won't be made to. There will be some sparring involved in your training, but this will take place under controlled supervision, and is just a standard part of training practice.

You will need a licence before you can begin training (your club will arrange this for you). This is a booklet that includes your insurance, and it will hold your grading record (if you wish to grade) and will also show your fight record (if you wish to compete).

Equipment

The clothing and equipment used in Thai Boxing is different to that of other martial arts such as Karate and Judo, as no suit (*gi*) is worn. Instead, students wear club shorts and a T-shirt. Also, anklets are worn to help keep the ankles strong.

Most clubs will probably look like your average boxing gym. There may also be a ring, where students will spar. The most common items of club equipment you are likely to come across are:

- The long pad: oblong-shaped pads that buckle around the forearm and wrist, used for kicks, elbow strikes, knee strikes and punches.
- The big pad, which is used for practising strong, thrust-type kicks.
- The heavy bag, used for strong punching.
- Focus mitts, used for punching combinations.

Training

Your training can be hard or easy: it's whatever you make it. Always try to give one hundred per cent when you train – there's no point practising half-heartedly.

A typical class will begin with the traditional bow, followed by a warm-up consisting of cardio work, maybe some running on the spot, star jumps, and so on, plus stretching exercises to cover head to toe. Once warmed up, you will be put through the basics. The class may or may not be split into groups, according to ability. Pad work is an important part of your training: hitting fresh air is fine if you're shadow boxing, but to throw a fully locked-out technique without meeting a target is not good for the joints. Also, hitting the pads will improve your speed, power and timing. You will also move through a number of combination techniques in your class, probably involving some fitness work, and maybe some light sparring. For the sparring work you will be padded up with protective equipment for your safety, so don't worry.

Above all, you should enjoy your training. Relax and train to the best of your ability, and you won't go far wrong.

Club rules

There are a number of basic rules that apply in all clubs, which all students must abide by.

- *Wai* (the bow) must be done:
  - –when entering and leaving your training area
  - –when joining a class
  - –to an instructor, when they ask you to do something
  - –to fellow students in class
- It is important that you are always clean and presentable, and that your club uniform is

clean. Your armband (which indicates your grade; *see Grading, right*) must be worn at all times.

- No jewellery is to be worn while training. No smoking in the club, and no alcohol before class.
- Respect must be shown to your instructor and fellow students.
- No disrespect is to be made of any other martial art.
- Students must never misuse their Thai Boxing training knowledge.

Grading

'Will I be able to grade?' is a question I'm often asked by students. The answer is, simply, 'Yes!' There are set syllabuses which differ slightly from association to association, and from one club to another, but again the basic principles still apply.

A grading will consist of the following: basics (which includes punching, kicking, elbowing and kneeing), grappling, combination work, sparring, defence work, pad work, terminology, history and Ram Muay. Although this may sound like a lot, you will be learning gradually as you progress in your training – you won't be expected to know all of the above for your first grade attempt! The more you put into your training, the more you will get out of it; you don't need to rush to attempt your next grade. To reach the level of Kru will take a good few years and hard training, but if this is your goal, do stick with it, as it is definitely worthwhile.

In Thai Boxing, the grades are recognized by armbands – the *Kruang Ruang*. These are coloured as follows:

1st Khan • *white*
2nd Khan • *yellow*
3rd Khan • *green*
4th Khan • *blue*
5th Khan • *blue and white*
6th Khan • *brown*
7th Khan • *brown and white*
8th Khan • *brown and yellow*
Assistant Kru • *brown and red*
Kru • *red*

To reach instructor level, students must have trained for a minimum of three to four years, and must also help out in classes and in the running of the club.

Terminology

The following is a quick guide to the most common Thai words you are likely to come across in your training. Don't worry – you won't be expected to be fluent in Thai, but you will find it useful to be familiar with a few basic terms, as some clubs use Thai when referring to their training techniques. You may also be required to know the Thai terminology for gradings (your club will inform you of this). Although pronunciation, as well as spelling, often differs between clubs (for example, note the two different ways of pronouncing 'Muay' given below), your basic grasp of common terms should be sufficient for you to understand – and be understood by – those that train in Thai Boxing.

If you are unsure of something, always ask what it means. Words may be spelled differently to how they sound, so always try to find out about the words you are using. The terms below include a basic phonetic guide to help you pronounce them correctly.

anklet *Aenken* (an-kun)
arm *Kaen* (kairn)
armband *Kruang Ruang* (croo-ang roo-ang)
block *Bat* (bad)
bow *Wai* (why)
bow to teacher *Wai Kru* (why croo)
boxer *Nak Muay* (nak moo-ee/m-why)
boxer's dance *Ram Muay* (ram moo-ee/m-why)
camp/club *Kai* (kye)
elbow *Sawk* (sore)
fist *Matt* (madt)
foot *Thao* (t-ow)
head *Hua* (hoo-a)
headband *Mongkon* (mong-kon)
hello *Sawadee* (saw-wat-dee)
instructor *Kru* (croo)
kick *Dteh* (deh)
knee *Kao* (cow)
leg *Kaa* (car)
stomach *Tong* (taang)
Thai Boxing *Muay Thai* (moo-ee/m-why tie)
throw *Ting* (ting)

NUMBERS
one *Nueng* (noong)
two *Sorng* (sorng)
three *Saam* (sarm)
four *See* (see)
five *Har* (haa)
six *Hok* (hohk)
seven *Ched* (jet)
eight *Paed* (paird)
nine *Gao* (kow)
ten *Sip* (sip)

Competition

Do you want to compete in fighting tournaments? This is something that many Thai Boxing students will consider as their training progresses (indeed, you may already have a fair idea of whether or not you're interested in the competition side of Thai Boxing before you take up the martial art). Remember: there is no obligation to compete, but if it's something you think you may be interested in, this will give you a general idea of what to expect.

There are a number of levels at which you can compete, and although these may vary slightly from country to country, generally you will find: inter-club competition, local competition, regional competition, national competition and title fights. Most fights are three to five rounds, and normally two to three minutes in duration, depending on the level at which you are competing. Some title fights may have more rounds, depending on who is sanctioning the event.

In competition, the following equipment is usually worn (again, you will find that this varies as you gain more experience and fight under different associations):

- Headguard
- Mouthpiece (gumshield)
- Body protection
- Shin and instep protection
- Handwraps
- Boxing gloves
- Groinguard

Fighting isn't easy. When you spar in training, you know that both you and your partner are students who train together; when you fight in a competition, most of the time you will have never seen your opponent before.

Training to fight requires one hundred per

cent focus. Nothing should distract you. Your coach will put in the extra time for you, so you should give the same in return. Your sleep, rest and diet are important, as is maintaining a good level of fitness: without it, you will find it hard in the ring. Fitness training will include roadwork (running), skipping, bag and pad work and good sparring rounds in your training sessions. The training will be harder than your regular sessions, but this will ultimately make your fighting easier. A good competitor is someone who goes out and tries their best – win, lose or draw. As long as you try, no one will doubt you.

I could go on and on with advice about competition, but each instructor will differ in the way they coach a fighter. Listen to your instructor: they will give you the best advice for *you*, and the tips you need to become a good fighter. If you are taking up Thai Boxing to become a fighter, I wish you the best of luck. Always remember, though, that not all the students who train at your club will want to compete, so respect them in the same way you respect your fellow fighters. You are all practitioners of the art of Thai Boxing.

About the book

The book is designed as a supplement to your training in class. Carry it around with you as a handy reference guide, so that you can practise your techniques whenever you get the chance. Don't feel that you have to work through the book in any particular order: you'll know which aspects of your technique you need to brush up on at any given time, so pick and choose sections as appropriate. Always read the top tips provided, as they'll help you to get the best results. And remember: regular training is the key to success, so practise, practise, practise.

BASIC ESSENTIALS

Warming up

The warm-up is a very important part of your training routine. It's vital to include exercises that warm the body from head to toe at the beginning of every training session. The selection of exercises shown here will get your body warm and get your pulse and heart rate going, as well as starting to stretch the body's muscles. Repeat each exercise a few times (unless otherwise stated).

▼ **NECK ROTATIONS** Stand with your feet shoulder width apart, hands on hips, back straight. Rotate your head slowly, first taking your chin to your chest, then back as far as possible. Next, from the centre, turn your head to look left then right, then tip your left ear to your left shoulder, and vice versa.

▲ **JOGGING ON THE SPOT** Begin by walking slowly on the spot, then gradually start to lift your legs a little more and move into a faster pace. Work your pace up to a jog on the balls of your feet, moving your arms up and down from waist to chest. Do this exercise for a couple of minutes.

▲ **ARM SWINGS** Swing your arms in a circular motion, crossing them over as you reach chest level. Repeat in opposite direction. This warms your arms and shoulders.

TOP TIP
The warm-up is essential to your routine. You can vary the exercises, but always include some light cardio work and stretching. Don't overdo it, or you will burn yourself out before you begin training. And remember to warm down at the end – this is just as important as warming up.

▲ **SIDE ARM SWINGS** Swing your arms across in front of your body at chest level, so your hands touch the sides of your upper body (alternate the uppermost arm with each swing), then swing them out to the sides. This warms the chest and upper back muscles.

▼ **HIP ROTATIONS** Standing with your feet shoulder width apart, hands on hips, rotate your hips in a circular motion, circling wider as you go, so that you come up onto the sides of your feet. Repeat in the opposite direction.

▲ **KNEE ROTATIONS** Stand with your hands closed into fists up by your shoulders. Lift one leg up in front of your stomach, knee just past waist height, then circle it across your body to your side. Repeat with opposite leg.

Stretching

Regular stretching will increase your overall flexibility and suppleness. Add these exercises to your warm-up. Start slowly, and try to stretch further as you go on.

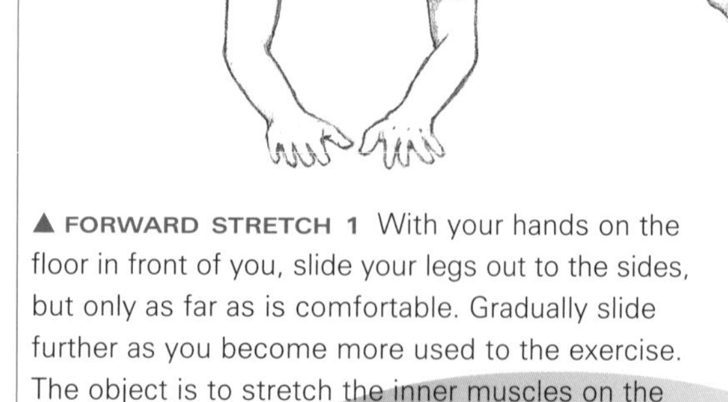

▲ **FORWARD STRETCH 1** With your hands on the floor in front of you, slide your legs out to the sides, but only as far as is comfortable. Gradually slide further as you become more used to the exercise. The object is to stretch the inner muscles on the upper leg and in the groin area.

▲ **SIDE LUNGE** Step out to the side with one leg, with your foot pointing outwards. Keeping your body straight, bend your front leg, pushing forward with your rear hip until you reach a parallel level. Don't stretch too far forward. Repeat on opposite side.

▲ **FORWARD STRETCH 2** This is the same as the above, but stretches more of the hamstring muscles. Stretch your arms as far forward as possible in front of you, then bring them back to the centre, and finally through your legs (if you can!).

◀ **FRONT LEG SWINGS** Stand with one leg in front of the other in a fighting stance, hands in a guard position. Let your rear leg swing in front of you, then back into your stance. Relax your leg and let it swing; don't kick.

TOP TIP
Always stretch before and after your training sessions. Make sure your body is fully warmed up before beginning your stretching, and don't bounce on your stretch. If you feel any pain while stretching, stop immediately.

▶ **SIDE LEG SWINGS** Stand with your feet shoulder width apart, hands held up in front of your chest. Swing your leg out to the side and back down to the floor. Repeat with the opposite side.

▲ **FRONT SPLITS STRETCH** Sit on the floor, legs as wide apart as possible, and try to turn your hips downwards. Bring your chest as close to the floor as you can, keeping your head up, as this will keep the spine straight.

▼ **SIDE SPLITS STRETCH** Turn to your side, place one leg out in front, and slide your back leg behind you as far as you can. Lean forward, touching your chest to your front leg; don't drop your head down.

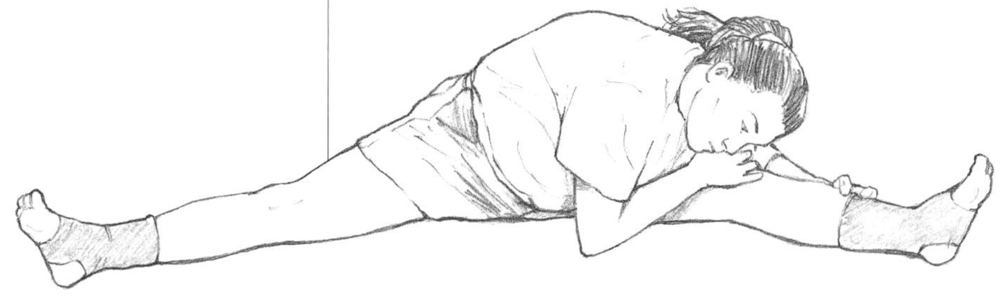

Bowing

The bow is one of the most important moves in your Thai Boxing training. It is courteous to bow to your *Kru* (instructor) and to fellow students. You must always bow in and out of your training class, and also when you are asked to do a movement in class.

1◀ Draw your right foot towards your left foot, keeping both feet together, and place both hands by your sides. Stand in a firm, upright position, facing forward and looking straight ahead.

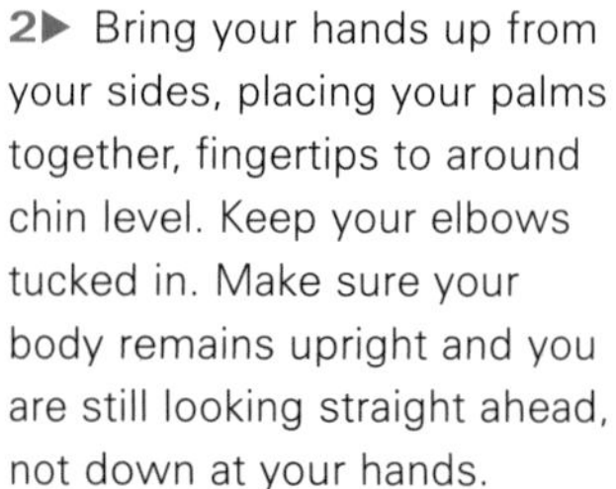

2▶ Bring your hands up from your sides, placing your palms together, fingertips to around chin level. Keep your elbows tucked in. Make sure your body remains upright and you are still looking straight ahead, not down at your hands.

◀ **HAND POSITION** When placing your palms together, your fingers and thumbs should be level, much the same as holding your hands together in a prayer position.

TOP TIP
The bow is done as one fluid movement and at a medium pace. Remember: always bow as you are entering or leaving a class, to a Kru, to a Senior, and when you are given an order in class.

3◀ Now bring your hands up in front of your nose, to around eyebrow level. Do this by sliding your hands in front of your face and then tipping your fingers back slightly to touch your head, between your eyebrows.

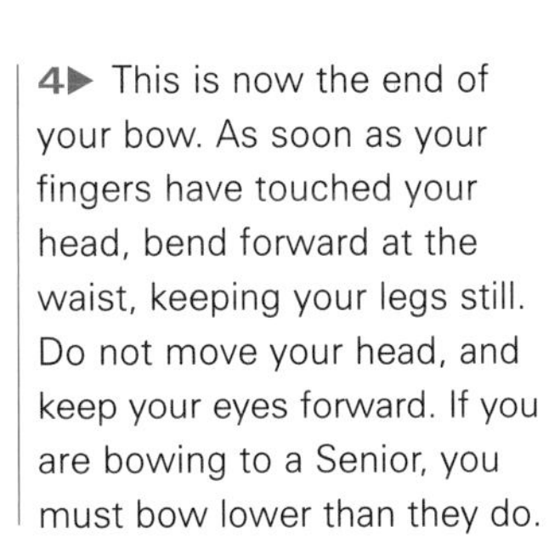

4▶ This is now the end of your bow. As soon as your fingers have touched your head, bend forward at the waist, keeping your legs still. Do not move your head, and keep your eyes forward. If you are bowing to a Senior, you must bow lower than they do.

Stances

The stances and guards of Thai Boxing vary slightly depending on the association, and also whether the stance is Eastern or Western. The basic principle, however, is always the same: one leg in front of the other, and hands up to guard the body and face.

STYLE A

▲ This is the most common stance. Stand with your feet shoulder width apart, front foot facing forward, back foot at roughly 45 degrees. Raise both hands (fists) in front of you, keeping your elbows in, but in a loose, comfortable position.

Side View 1

Notice the position of the feet. Try to stay on the balls of your feet by rocking slowly forwards and backwards on your toes, from foot to foot.

Side View 2

Here you can clearly see the curve in the spine. With your hands held high up in the guard position, relax your neck, and lift and round your shoulders forward a little, so that your back feels slightly hunched.

STYLE B

▼ This stance is more traditional, and favored by Bangkok camps (clubs). The set-up is similar to Style A, except the front hand is now further forward, in front of the body.

Side View 1
This angle shows how far the lead guarding arm has come out. Your body and legs should be in the same position as for Style A, but this time both arms come further forward, away from your body, with the front guarding arm stretched out (but not fully – keep a slight bend at the elbow).

TOP TIP

It's not set in stone that you have to copy the main stances exactly; we're all built differently, so find a stance that suits you. Try aspects of both stances, until you find a comfortable position.

PUNCHES

Jab

The jab and the cross (*see right*) are the two most basic punches used in Thai Boxing. Notice the straightness of the jab.

TOP TIP
Don't drop the non-punching hand – always keep this as a guarding hand. Never over-commit on your punching. Keep relaxed until the point of impact; if you are too tense, you will lose power and speed from your punch.

1▲ Start off in your normal fighting stance, body nice and relaxed, guard held high. You can move your arms around very slightly, but don't let them drop down in front of you.

2▼ Begin to shift some weight onto your front leg: this will stabilize you, so that your jab will be strong. Notice that the shoulder and arm have not dropped.

3▶ Now push more weight from the back leg, and rotate the shoulder of your punching arm, to give you greater range. Fully extend your arm to the target.

Target area

Cross

Concentrate on the twist of the body as you perform the cross.

1▲ Start as you did for the jab, in normal fighting stance, hands held high, body relaxed, and weight balanced between front and rear leg. Again, a little light movement is OK, but make sure you are stable just as you are going to throw your punch.

2▲ Begin to rotate your rear hip forward, coming up onto the ball of your rear foot. Using your shoulder and upper back muscles, start to extend your rear arm slightly across the body.

3▼ Now throw the weight from twisting, using your rear hip, to deliver the punch, coming right up onto the ball of your rear foot. Extend your arm fully to the target area. Do not throw this punch straight out or throw your body around fully.

Uppercut

This punch, and the hook that follows, work best close into the body. They can be body or head shots.

TOP TIP
Note how the hips move into a punch to generate the power and drive. Keep your movement smooth, as this will improve the speed of your technique. Always return to your full guard once you have delivered your punch.

1◀ Begin in a stance that is slightly square on. This allows you to transfer the weight easily from the left to the right side of your body, and vice versa, by swaying the upper body from side to side.

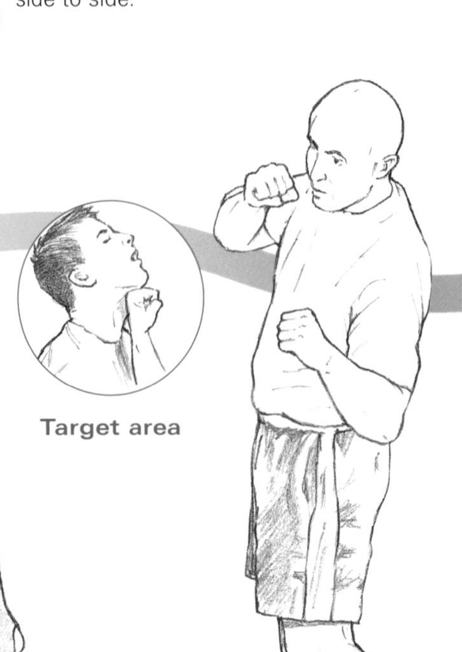

Target area

2▶ Start to transfer your weight onto your left side by tipping your upper body sideways, bending your left leg, and dropping your lead arm down a little, so that your elbow is roughly in line with your waist.

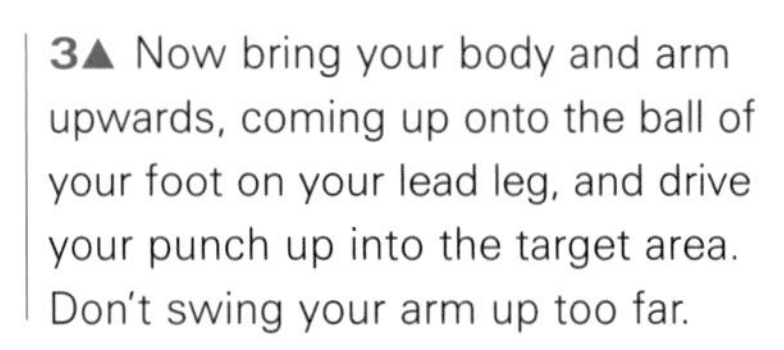

3▲ Now bring your body and arm upwards, coming up onto the ball of your foot on your lead leg, and drive your punch up into the target area. Don't swing your arm up too far.

Hook

The uppercut and hook are normally used as short punches to knock an opponent with, or used in combination, in a flurry of techniques.

1◀ Back in your normal fighting stance, with your hands held high, keep your body and shoulders relaxed and your weight distributed evenly, so that you will be able to rotate your hips in either direction.

2▶ Draw your rear arm out towards the side, coming up onto the ball of your rear foot, and beginning to twist your hip from the rear.

3▲ Now rotate your hip and arm simultaneously, letting your punch come through. Don't over-extend: you must be able to swing your hips back, either to continue with a combination or return to your stance.

STRIKES

Roundhouse elbow strike

The elbows are a very effective striking tool. This strike is also known as the cutting elbow.

TOP TIP
Always keep your arms in a guarding position, so that you are ready to follow up with further elbow strikes or punches. Remember: your shoulders *must* be relaxed for you to throw maximum effort into your elbow strikes.

1▼ Stand in your front fighting stance. You can either move slowly around your target or stay in the same spot. Relax your shoulders, as you are about to use them to execute your attack.

2◀ Lift your rear arm up to around shoulder level, coming up onto the ball of your rear foot, ready to shift your weight into your attacking technique. At the same time, open your front hand: this will guard you more against your opponent, as you are moving close in.

Target area

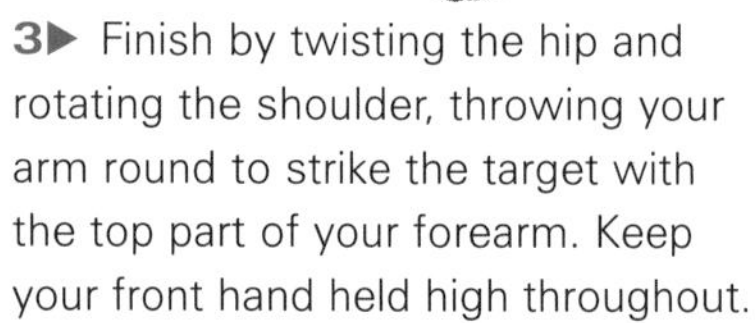

3▶ Finish by twisting the hip and rotating the shoulder, throwing your arm round to strike the target with the top part of your forearm. Keep your front hand held high throughout.

Rising elbow strike

Elbow strikes are delivered in a similar way to punches, in that they incorporate hip, leg and body movement.

1▲ From your fighting stance, open your lead hand and keep your rear hand closed: this will cover you if your opponent moves in before you have the chance to throw your strike.

2▼ Drop your body weight down from your rear leg by bending at the knee, but don't drop too far, or you will find that you have to jump up into your strike. Begin raising your rear arm, in readiness for the delivery.

Target area

3▲ Continue to lift your rear arm up to come into your strike, while at the same time bringing your front arm down to around chest level. This will give you more drive and power in your elbow technique.

Downward elbow strike

This technique is perhaps the most powerful of all the elbow strikes. It can cause considerable damage, so must only be practised using an appropriate training pad. *Do not* practise it on a fellow student.

TOP TIP
This technique is very effective as a means of self-defence, due to its devastating power. Remember: it should never be practised on another student.

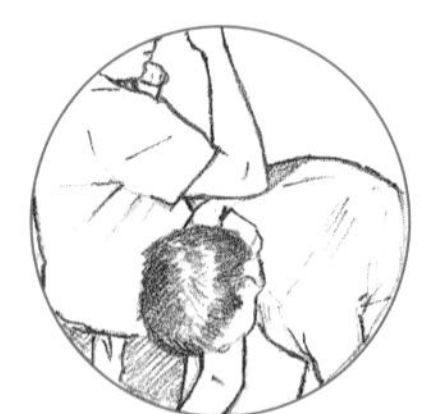

Target area

2▶ Lift your rear arm up, fist slightly clenched (similar to a hammer-fist type movement), pulling your front arm across your body and opening your hand, in readiness to block any oncoming attack.

1▲ As with the rising elbow and roundhouse elbow, start this technique in your normal fighting stance. Keep your arms in a guard position, ready to move into your attack.

3▼ Continue raising your rear attacking arm, stretching up as high as possible, but keeping a 45-degree bend in the arm. Lower your front arm down to around stomach level, and come up on your back leg – right up onto the ball of your foot.

5▼ Finish your attack by driving the elbow point into the target area, bending at the knees to enable you to move closer into your opponent. As you drive your attacking arm down, bring your front arm back up to a guarding position.

4▲ Now begin to bring your attacking arm downwards into the technique. Just as you lowered your front arm to maintain your centre of balance while raising the rear attacking arm, now start to bring it back up, as the rear arm begins to strike downwards.

Roundhouse knee strike

The knees are a very powerful tool in the Thai Boxing practitioner's arsenal. They are used in many striking arts, but are a speciality of Thai Boxing.

2▼ Begin to lift your rear leg up to the side, pulling your calf in as close as possible to your buttocks. Keep your hands in the 'grab' position throughout.

1▼ Throw out both arms as if you are grabbing hold of someone around the back of the neck. Come up onto the ball of your rear foot and prepare to turn your right hip into the movement.

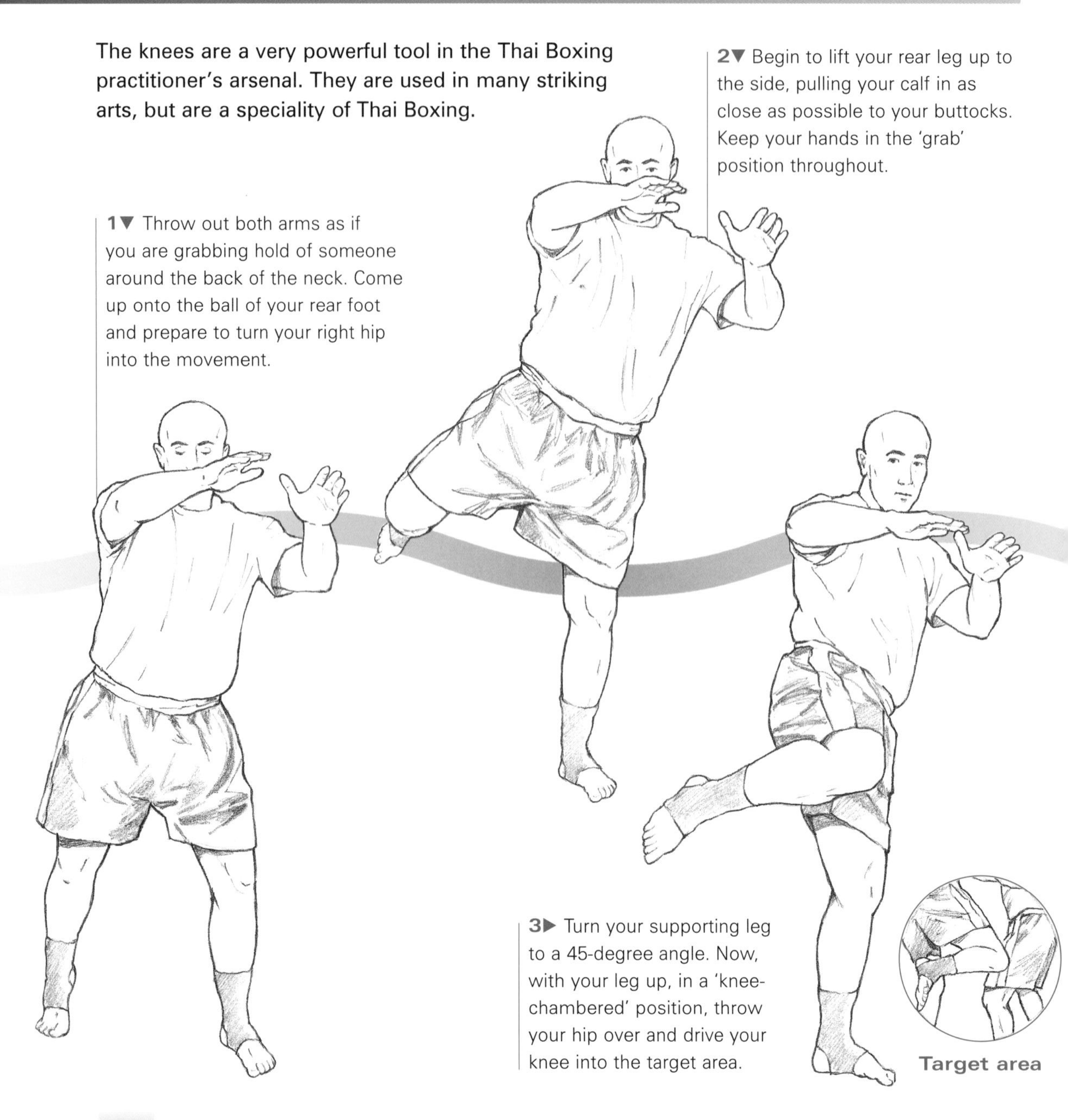

3▶ Turn your supporting leg to a 45-degree angle. Now, with your leg up, in a 'knee-chambered' position, throw your hip over and drive your knee into the target area.

Target area

Rising knee strike

Knee strikes can be aimed at various parts of the body, to devastating effect.

1▲ As before, throw your arms up in a 'grabbing' position, but this time at around head height. As you do this, step up onto the ball of your rear foot.

2▲ Begin to raise your leg, again keeping the calf as close as possible to the buttocks, but this time keep your toes pointing down towards to the floor. Start to lower your hand position (equivalent to your opponent's head).

3▼ Thrust your rear hip forward, leaning back slightly to give you the drive you need for a good technique. Simultaneously, draw your arms back down, as if pulling your opponent's head in towards you.

> **TOP TIP**
> **Always pull the calf as close to the buttocks as you can, as this makes for a stronger technique. Don't forget to lean back slightly for the rising knee, so you can drive through with the strike.**

Side knee strike

This is also known as the slap knee – and you will find out why when you do it! It may just look like a leg swing exercise, but once you have received one of these strikes you will believe its power.

1◀ From your fighting stance, throw your arms up as if to make a grab for the back of your opponent's neck. Come up onto the ball of the foot on the rear leg.

2▲ Pull your elbows in, so as to tighten the hold you have on your opponent. Begin to lift the rear leg up, bending the knee, with the inside of the thigh facing outwards.

TOP TIP
Look at the point of impact. Do not use the top of the knee. Make sure you use your hip to drive the striking leg across; don't throw your leg too far around when you raise it, or your strike will be insufficiently 'loaded'.

3▲ Now, with your front foot still pointing forward, throw your rear leg up and out to the side. Don't throw it out too far, or with too much power, as this will unbalance you.

4▶ Finish by pulling your arms across your body to the side (effectively pulling your opponent into the attack), while at the same time throwing your leg back across your body, using your hip to drive your knee into the target area. The hip generates the power in this technique.

KICKS

Front kicks

Here we have two variations of the front kick. One uses the whole of the foot to push an opponent back in a thrusting motion, while the other is good for working into a smaller area, in a snapping motion. To a beginner, both kicks may seem similar at first, but once you have gained some experience you will soon learn when to use each one.

PUSH KICK

1▼ From your guard stance, lift your front leg into a chambered position, leaning back slightly – but not too far, or you will overbalance.

2▲ Now throw your leg out in front of you, in a thrusting motion, pushing into your opponent's midriff area. As you do this, lean back a little further, to increase the drive and power of your kick.

SNAP KICK

1▼ Begin as you did for the push kick, but this time lift your knee up as high as possible, as you will be kicking to head height.

2▲ Now kick up towards the target area by extending your leg from the chambered position, using the ball of your foot to strike your target. Don't lean back in this kick, as you will not get the height that you are after.

TOP TIP

Remember: lean back on your push kick, but *keep upright* on your snap kick, and use the ball of the foot for the snap. Keep your guard throughout.

Roundhouse kicks

The roundhouse kick is a popular kick in most striking martial arts but, unlike the kicks used in arts such as Karate and Taekwondo, in Thai Boxing you don't snap back to a chambered position, instead bringing your kicking leg straight back down to land on the floor. Also, you can use either the shin or the instep part of your foot.

SHIN

1◀ Begin in your fighting stance, hands held high in guard position, ready to lift your rear leg towards your kicking position.

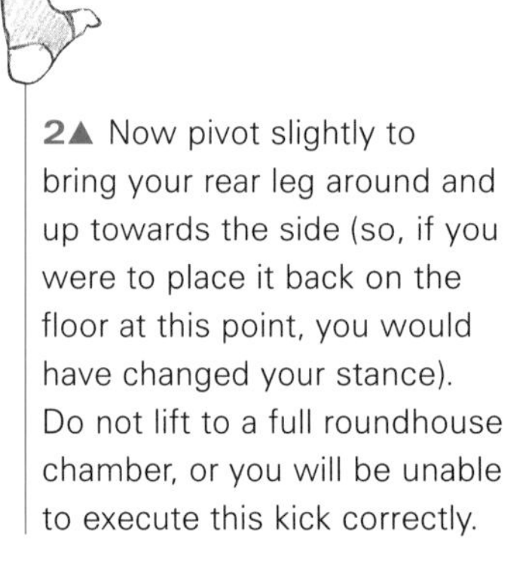

2▲ Now pivot slightly to bring your rear leg around and up towards the side (so, if you were to place it back on the floor at this point, you would have changed your stance). Do not lift to a full roundhouse chamber, or you will be unable to execute this kick correctly.

3▼ Finish by throwing the leg round, rotating on the ball of the foot on your supporting leg. The speed and power of this kick is generated by the way it is swung from the hips. Do not snap the kick out. This kick can be used to strike high, middle and low areas.

TOP TIP

Remember to use your hip to throw the kicking leg round, to ensure maximum power, and always land straight back down on the floor – don't snap the kick out and back. Note the impact points for both kicks.

FOOT/INSTEP

▲ The technique is the same as for the shin kick, except this time lift your front leg from your fighting stance, and throw it round on a low level. You are aiming to strike with the instep: when connected correctly with the target, it should make a slapping sound.

Side kick

The side kick and back kick (*see right*) are normally – and best – used when struck to an opponent's midsection. Using these kicks above chest height will restrict the power in the technique.

TOP TIP
Always keep your eyes on your target when you turn to do the back kick. Remember: the heel can reach a small target, while the flat of the foot is best for pushing an opponent back.

1◄ From your fighting stance turn sideways on, rotating slightly on the back foot and keeping your guard. Lift the front leg, turning your front foot so the sole is parallel with your target, ready to throw the leg to kick out.

2◄ Now thrust your leg out towards the midsection, using the combined momentum of pulling your arms up towards your chest while pushing your hips forwards. This drives the power of the movement.

Back kick

Both the back kick and the side kick (*see left*) use a powerful thrusting motion; use them to keep an opponent at bay or push them back.

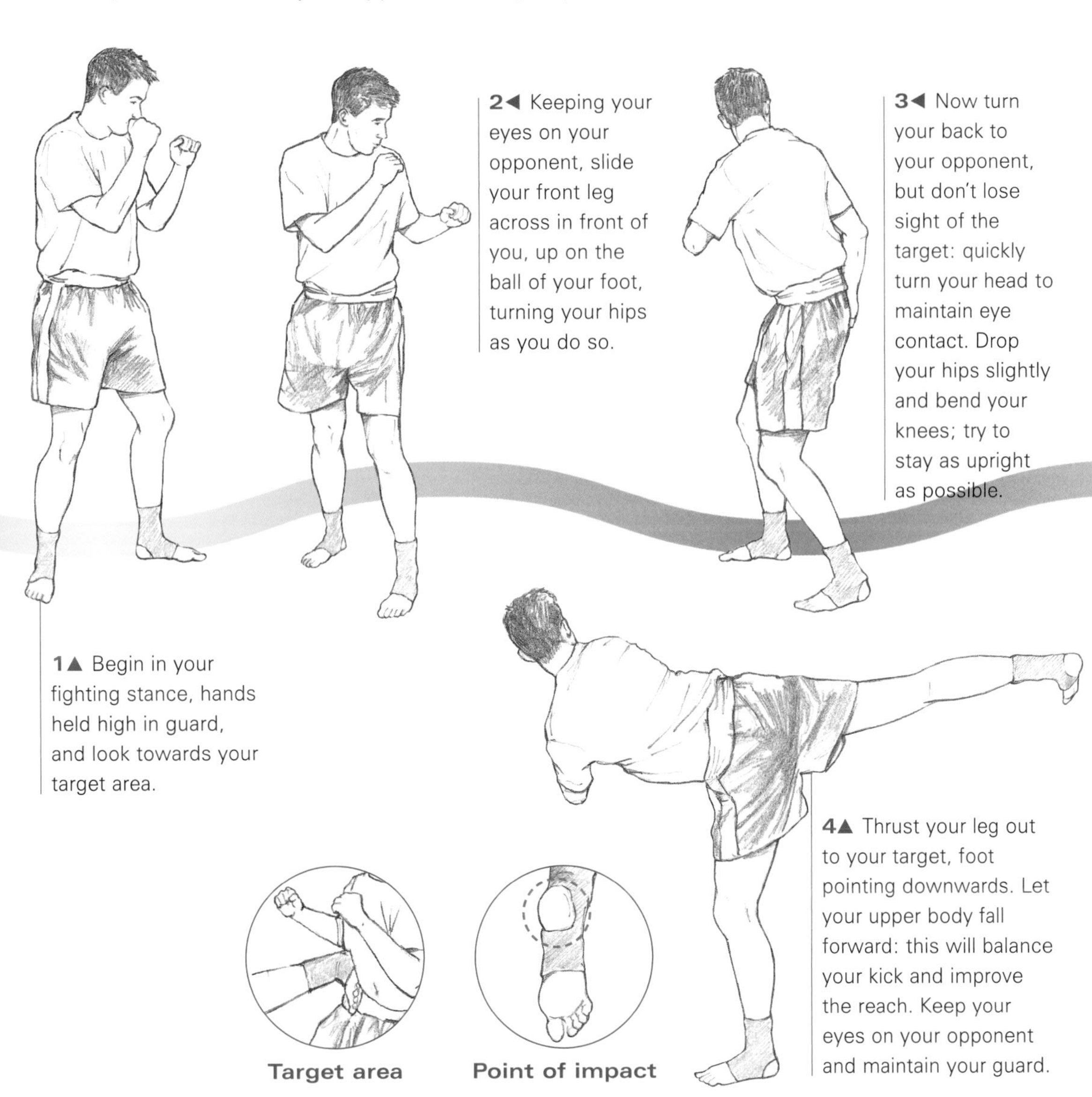

1▲ Begin in your fighting stance, hands held high in guard, and look towards your target area.

2◀ Keeping your eyes on your opponent, slide your front leg across in front of you, up on the ball of your foot, turning your hips as you do so.

3◀ Now turn your back to your opponent, but don't lose sight of the target: quickly turn your head to maintain eye contact. Drop your hips slightly and bend your knees; try to stay as upright as possible.

4▲ Thrust your leg out to your target, foot pointing downwards. Let your upper body fall forward: this will balance your kick and improve the reach. Keep your eyes on your opponent and maintain your guard.

Target area

Point of impact

Hook kick

The hook kick is known in some martial arts as the reverse roundhouse. It can use either the heel or the ball of the foot.

TOP TIP
Remember to lean back on the spinning hook kick, as this will give you better height, and whip your kick round fast for maximum power. The heel is ideal for striking small target areas, and will sink into the body better than other parts of the foot.

1▲ From the guard, turn sideways on, lifting your front leg in readiness to swing the whole leg up the side of your opponent, to just before the target area.

2▲ Having swung your leg up into position, continue the movement by bringing your foot across the face (*see target area*). This is done by whipping the lower part of the leg across, slapping the target with the ball of your foot.

Spinning hook kick

The spinning hook, when connected correctly and with great speed, can knock an opponent out, due to the combined power from the spin and the whipping-round action of the leg.

1◀ From your guard stance, move your rear leg forward, similar to a changed stance (where you swap the leading leg) but turning the foot slightly inwards, which will give you your spin. Look over your shoulder.

Target area

Point of impact

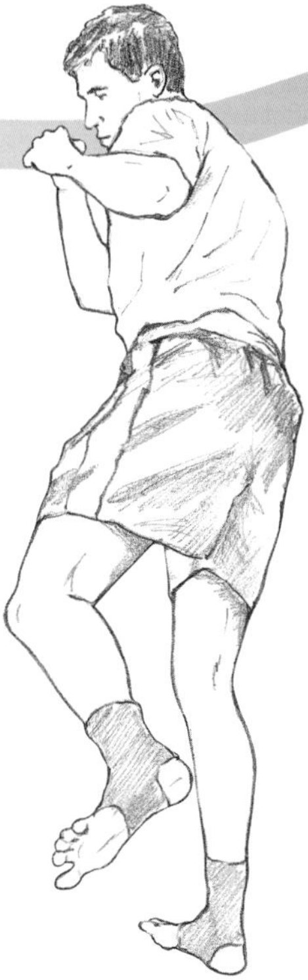

2▶ Begin to rotate your body around to your left, bending your right leg a little. Lift your left leg as you are turning, and this will start to give you the momentum to carry the kick through.

3▲ Continue the rotating movement, whipping your body round quickly, and leaning back to bring your raised leg up higher and give you a better swing on the kick. You are aiming to make contact with your heel.

BLOCKS

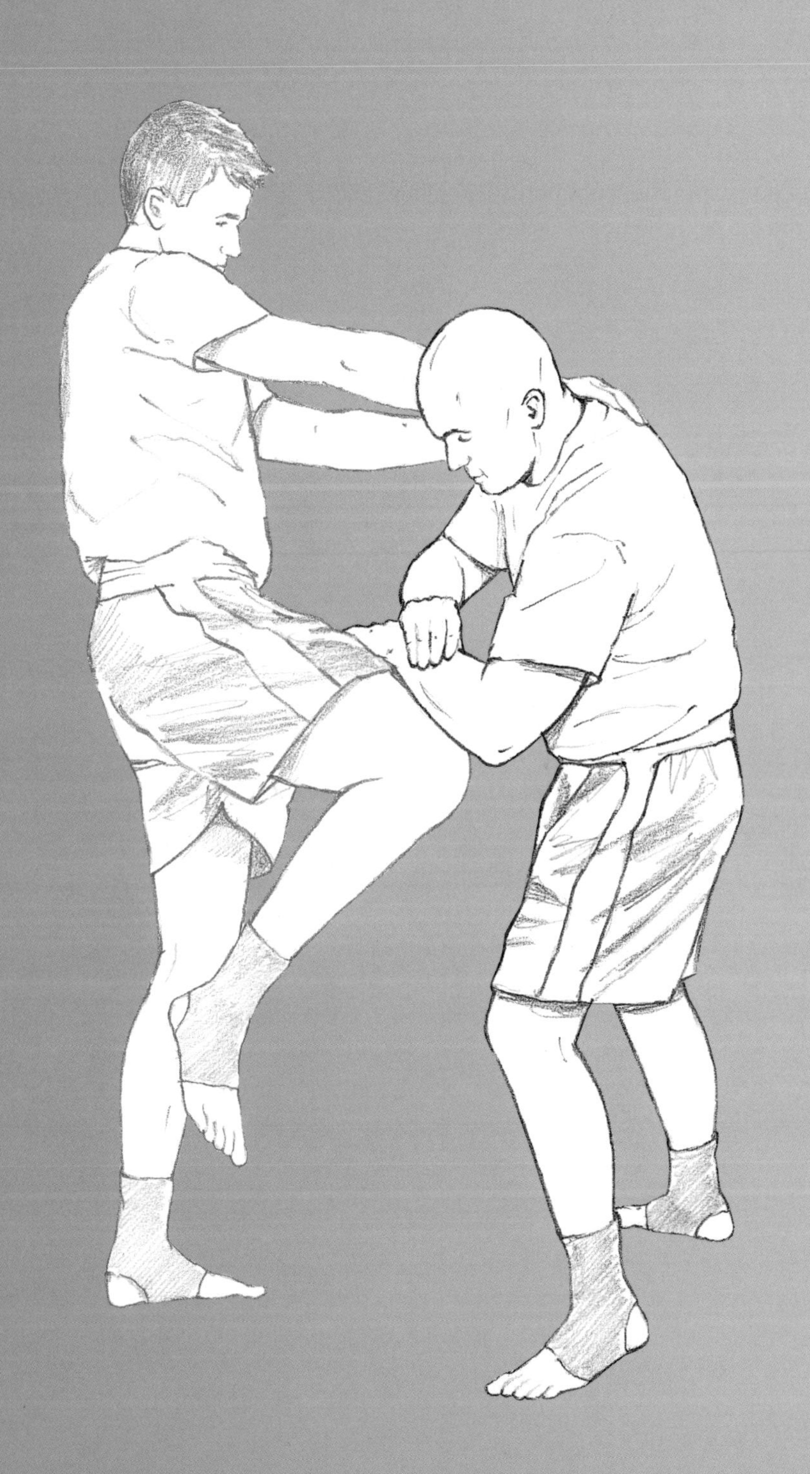

Rear hand parry

The rear hand parry and the front hand parry (*see right*) are used for the jab and the cross (*see pages 24–5*).

2▼ Now connect your parry with the jabbing hand and just tip it past you, in a slapping-type movement, bringing your hand straight back to the guarding position, ready to counter the attack.

1▲ As you see the attacker start to throw his jab, lean back slightly and tip your head a little to the right, raising your rear arm and opening your hand.

Front hand parry

These parries are simple slap-like blocks, rather than big sweeping movements, so don't be tempted to overdo them.

TOP TIP

Always lean out of the punch, whether slightly back, to the left or to the right. Don't sweep the attack out of the way, as this is likely to overbalance you, giving your opponent the chance to move in with another rapid-fire attack.

1▲ As with the rear hand parry (*see left*), watch the attack coming in. Lean your body back, lifting your front hand and keeping your rear hand in a guard position.

2▶ Slap into the attacking hand and rotate your body a little to the right. Don't bang the attack downwards, or you will lose your guard and leave yourself open to a rapid follow-up attack. From this move you should be able to counter-attack quickly.

Forearm blocks

These blocking techniques use the outside and inside of the forearm to stop an attack. The high block is a single-arm block using a simple lifting motion, normally used to stop rounding techniques. The low block uses both arms in a pushing-downward movement, and is best used for rising mid-level techniques.

2▲ Continue raising your arm until your open hand is touching your ear, so that, by the time the punch reaches you, you are able to absorb the impact with the outside of your forearm. Remember to tense your blocking arm at the moment of impact.

HIGH FOREARM BLOCK

1▲ Wait until you see the attack coming round, then move your upper body slightly forward, lifting up your front arm and opening your hand.

TOP TIP

For a successful block, always tense your blocking arm (or arms) as the attack makes impact. When blocking a knee attack, be sure to lean out of the attack as you are blocking.

LOW FOREARM BLOCK

1▼ Your attacker has grabbed you to attack you with a knee technique. Cross your arms by putting your right arm on top of your left, and bring them up to your chest area, in preparation for the block.

2▲ As the knee rises, push your forearms down to meet the attack, pushing your hips back at the same time. This will move your upper body away from the attack and leave you free to follow up with a counter.

Front leg shin block

Done correctly, this blocking technique will stop a low-leg roundhouse attack. If your shin connects with your attacker's shin, you'll discover that it's a very painful experience, so it's vital to make sure you block using the correct part of the leg.

TOP TIP
Remember to circle the blocking leg across the body – don't just move it up and down. Maintain your guard throughout; your attacker may switch from low to high roundhouse attack at the last minute.

1▲ When you see the roundhouse attack coming, from your stance start to lift your front leg up in front of you.

2▶ As the kick comes round, continue lifting the front blocking leg so that it stops the attack with the outside of the lower leg. Quickly tense your leg just as the kick makes impact, and then relax it again straight afterwards.

3▲ Now, having stopped the kick, push the roundhouse attack away by swinging your leg outwards to your left (much as you would in a knee rotation warm-up exercise).

4▶ Land back into your fighting stance, leaving you ready and able to follow up immediately with a counter technique, while your attacker is still in a vulnerable, unbalanced position.

Front kick block/leg catch

These are blocks/catches that allow you to keep hold of your opponent's attacking leg, so that you can then move in with your own counter technique. The first block can also be used to stop a roundhouse kick to the body, but here it is shown being used against a push/snap kick technique.

FRONT KICK BLOCK/CATCH

1▲ From your fighting stance, you see your opponent ready to throw a rear push or snap kick. Position your front guarding arm ready to block the attacking leg.

2▲ Just before the kick reaches its target, scoop your guarding arm down and under the leg, ready to pull the leg into your body. Keep your rear guarding arm ready to either block or counter.

3▶ Now pull the leg into your body, tucking it under your armpit, with the back of your hand pushing outwards against the side of the shin. You can follow this up with a rear-leg low kick.

2▼ Just as the kick is about to make impact, catch it with your rear hand, turning your hips slightly to the right, to unbalance your attacker.

FRONT KICK CATCH/PUSH

1▲ When you see your opponent lift his front leg to kick you, push your hips back to increase your distance from the attack. Open your hands, keeping a guard.

TOP TIP

When you catch the front leg kick, remember to pull the foot into your chest/ stomach area as you push your body forward, to leave your opponent vulnerable to a follow-up attack.

3◀ Now step forward, changing your stance. Pull the foot into your chest and push yourself forward. You can either throw the leg away or attack with a kick.

GRAPPLING

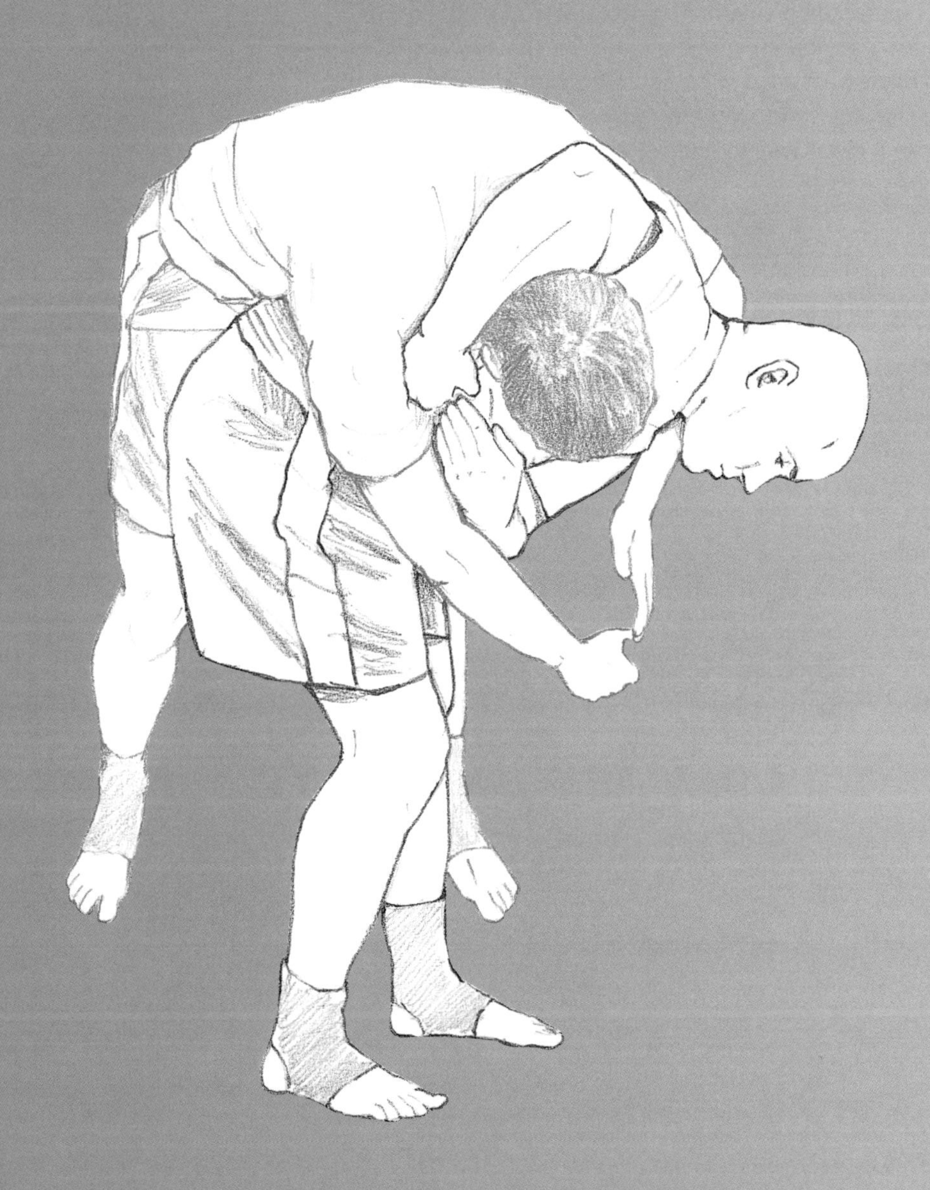

Clinch work

The grappling side of Thai Boxing is also known as clinch work and, in some clubs, neck wrestling. Clinch work is best used in conjunction with knee strikes, and is the way to move in to throw your opponent. It is also a great way to control your attacker.

TOP TIP
Remember to pull in tight once you have your opponent in the clinch. From this position, you can control your attacker and your knee strikes will be particularly effective.

2▼ Next, feed your left arm up through the guard, placing your left hand on top of the right, and pull your opponent onto you.

1▲ Feed your right arm through your opponent's guard, putting your hand on the back of his neck, and start to pull him into you.

3▲ Now push your forearms and elbows into your opponent's chest and force down on their neck, bringing their head onto your shoulder.

4▼ Finish by pulling the head tight into your shoulder, placing the side of your head on the side of his, and pull your arms in tighter so that your opponent's head is locked betwen your head and shoulder. You are now ready to deliver a good knee strike.

The clinch

Clinch and throw

There are a few basic throws that you can use in your grappling work, but here we look at a neck throw, as this is an easy one to do straight from the clinch. In a competition, a good way to finish is to land on your opponent, to take the wind out them. Not everyone likes to throw, but, more so, *no one* likes to be thrown.

1▲ Your opponent has you in the start of a clinch. Before he is able to get you in a full clinch, pull yourself back and immediately feed your right arm up and through, grabbing the base of his head.

2▲ Now feed your left arm through and straighten up your body, attempting to pull your opponent's head onto you. This will make him pull his head back up, away from you.

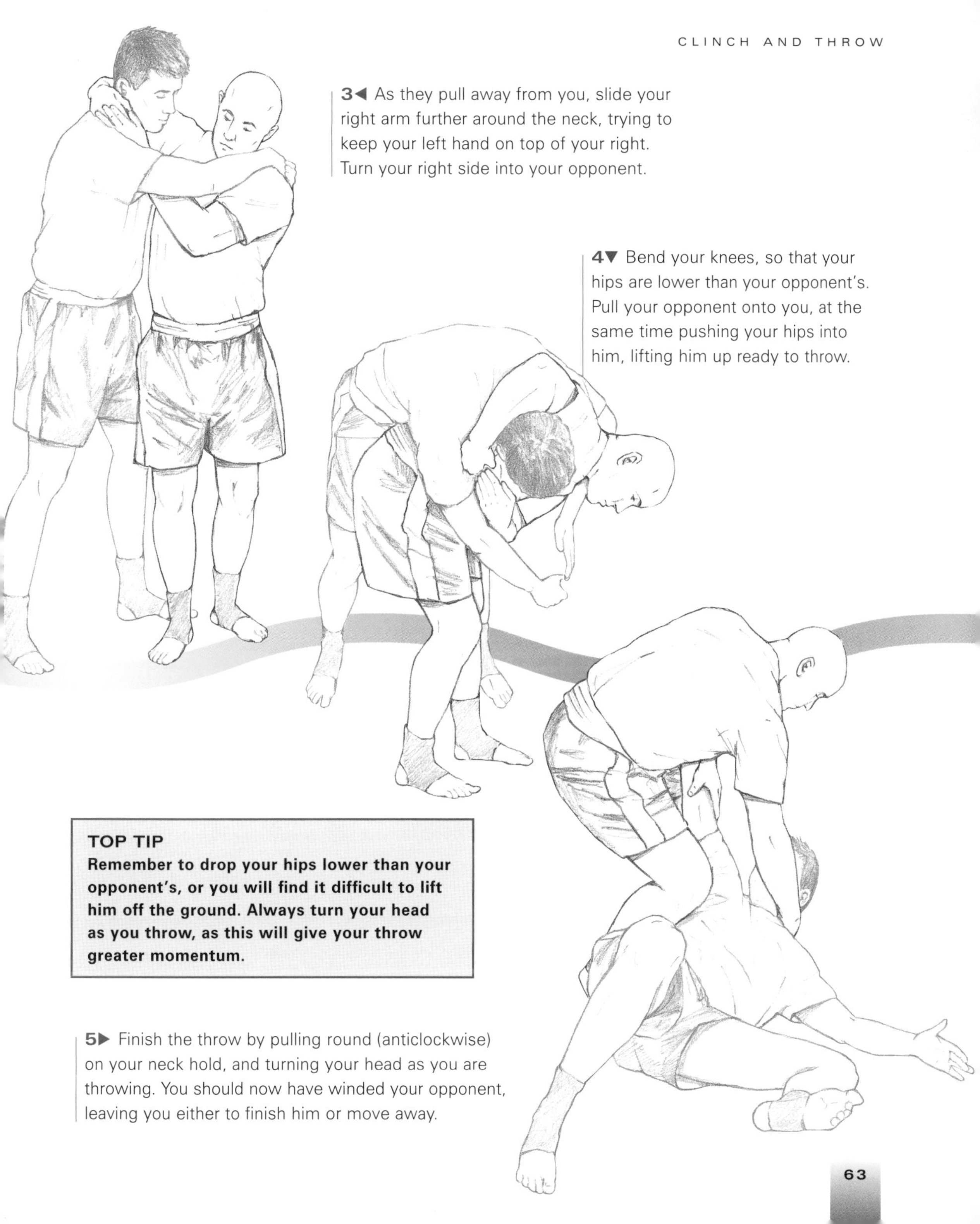

3◀ As they pull away from you, slide your right arm further around the neck, trying to keep your left hand on top of your right. Turn your right side into your opponent.

4▼ Bend your knees, so that your hips are lower than your opponent's. Pull your opponent onto you, at the same time pushing your hips into him, lifting him up ready to throw.

TOP TIP
Remember to drop your hips lower than your opponent's, or you will find it difficult to lift him off the ground. Always turn your head as you throw, as this will give your throw greater momentum.

5▶ Finish the throw by pulling round (anticlockwise) on your neck hold, and turning your head as you are throwing. You should now have winded your opponent, leaving you either to finish him or move away.

COMBINATION WORK

Combination 1

Jab/Roundhouse elbow/Rising knee

In this sequence of techniques you begin at a distance from your opponent, then move in closer at each stage, to finish with a knee strike. These three strikes flow well together to form this attacking combination.

2▼ Continue moving in with your attack, lifting your jabbing hand back to the guard position while simultaneously throwing a rear roundhouse elbow strike to the side of your opponent's head.

1▲ From your guard position, start moving in to your opponent as you throw out your left arm in a jab. Don't let the other guarding arm drop.

TOP TIP

From the jab, move straight in with your elbow strike – don't hesitate. Remember to pull your opponent into you as you are executing your knee strike, for maximum effect.

4▼ Finally, from the clinch, pull your opponent downwards, then drive your rear leg upwards into her midsection, in a rising knee strike.

3▲ After delivering the elbow strike, grab your opponent into a clinch by placing your hands on the back of her neck, remembering to place hand on top of hand (do *not* interlock your fingers, or you may end up injuring them).

Combination 2
Jab/Cross/Roundhouse kick

This combination puts together two punches and a kick. The punches are delivered from your normal fighting stance position – you do not move forwards in this attack.

2▼ As you are pulling back your jabbing arm, twist your rear hip forward, coming up onto the ball of your foot on your rear leg, and throw out your rear arm into a cross punch.

1▲ Stand in your normal fighting stance, guard held high. As you see your opponent move in, remain in your stance and push out your leading arm, to jab to your opponent's head.

3▶ Pull away from your opponent by stepping back with your rear leg and sliding your front leg back. Maintain your guard, with your rear hand held high and your front hand around chest level.

TOP TIP
Make sure you are standing in a firm stance when you throw your jab and cross. Remember to use your instep, and not your shin, for the roundhouse kick.

4▶ To finish, lean back and lift up your front leg to throw a low roundhouse kick to the inside of your opponent's leg. Use the instep part of your foot when you execute this kick.

Combination 3

Hook/Rising elbow/Rising knee/Roundhouse kick

This rather relentless combination sees a close-in attack using a punch and elbow strike immediately followed by a grab and knee strike, with a high kick to finish off.

1▲ From your fighting stance, move into your opponent and throw a front hand hook punch to the side of his face. Keep your rear hand up high, guarding throughout.

2▶ Now move in closer by sliding in off your front leg and coming up onto the ball of your rear foot, throwing a rising elbow strike under your opponent's chin as you do so.

3▲ Next, place your hands firmly on both shoulders of your opponent. Don't grab around the neck, as you would for the clinch.

4◀ Pull your opponent down towards you, push your hips back and throw a rear leg rising knee strike, leaning back slightly to increase the drive of your attack.

TOP TIP

Remember that you *do not* use the clinch hold when you grab your opponent for the knee strike. Don't forget to lean back into the knee strike for a stronger technique.

5▲ Now step back from your knee strike, bringing your striking leg back down to land behind you, while at the same time pushing your opponent by the shoulders, to move him away from you.

6▶ To finish the combination, twist on the ball of your front foot and throw your rear leg around to land with a roundhouse kick to the head, using the instep part of your foot.

Combination 4
Jab/Cross/Spinning back kick

This sequence features a double-punch attack, followed by a step back to draw your opponent onto a very powerful spinning back kick. Once you have stepped back, you must spin quickly to execute your kick; if you are too slow, you give your opponent time to close you down.

3▶ Pull back, away from your opponent, keeping your guard held high. As you pull back, turn your body sideways on to him, but keep your eyes on your target.

1▲ Move forward into your opponent and throw a front hand jab to his head. Keep your rear hand held high, ready for your next punch.

2▶ Straight after your jab, continue moving in (but don't swap your stance) and throw a rear cross punch to the head, rotating your hips as you do so.

TOP TIP
Don't pull too far back after you have delivered both punches; this will give you greater power in the thrust of your kick.

5▲ As your opponent moves in, throw out your spinning back kick straight into their midsection, to send them backwards. After executing the kick, pull your leg back and immediately return to your guard position.

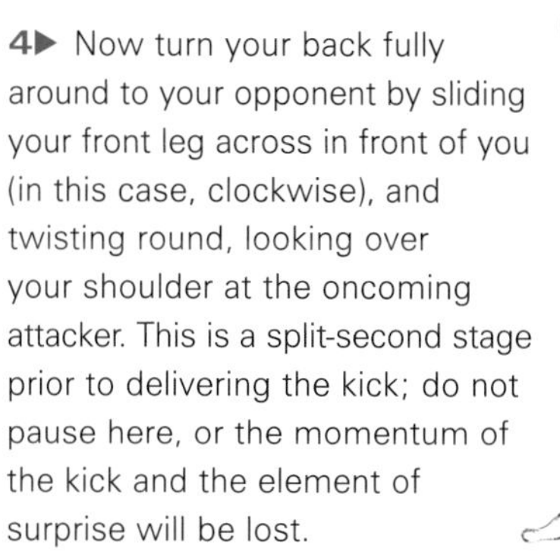

4▶ Now turn your back fully around to your opponent by sliding your front leg across in front of you (in this case, clockwise), and twisting round, looking over your shoulder at the oncoming attacker. This is a split-second stage prior to delivering the kick; do not pause here, or the momentum of the kick and the element of surprise will be lost.

Combination 5

Block/Jab/Front push kick

This combination involves a block and punch/kick counter. You must counter with your jab as soon as you have blocked, to stop your opponent from quickly following up with a second punch.

2▼ After you have parried the jab, counter the punch with a front hand jab strike to the face, preventing your opponent from coming in with another punching combination.

1▲ As you see your opponent attacking with a jab, block it with a rear hand parry. Move your head back out of the way of this attack.

3▲ Now lean back, lifting up your front leg, chambering for a front kick. Don't lean too far back, or you will overbalance. Keep a high guard.

4▼ Finish by thrusting your chambered leg, using a push kick, out towards the midsection of your attacker. Lean back to give you more thrust in your kick.

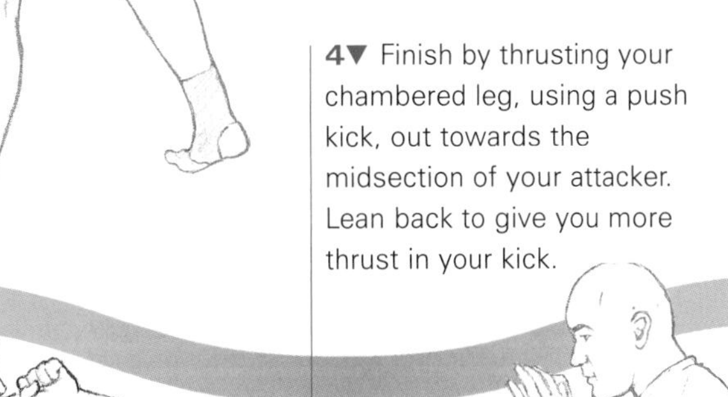

TOP TIP

Remember to counter as soon as you have blocked the jab, so that you don't lose your advantage. As your jab is on its way back, chamber your leg, ready to push your kick out.

Combination 6
Block/Roundhouse kick

This sequence focuses on the shin, using a low shin block to stop the attack, followed by an inside low roundhouse kick, using the shin as the striking point. The block will unbalance your opponent, allowing you to move in quickly with your counter technique.

TOP TIP
Make sure you use the shin, and not the instep, on the roundhouse kick, as this will give your kick greater power, and you will more likely fell your opponent as a result.

1▲ The attacker throws a rear leg low roundhouse. Block this with your front leg, using the shin block; this will knock your attacker off balance, leaving you to follow up with your counter.

2▶ Bring your blocking leg back down to land in front of you, resuming your normal fighting stance and keeping your eyes on your opponent.

3◀ Now begin to pull your front leg back, in readiness for your counter attack, but don't pull it too far or your opponent will have sufficient time to regain his balance and continue his attack.

4▶ Bring your leg forward and around, into a low roundhouse kick to the inside of the attacker's rear leg, using the shin. This will either fell your opponent or – at the very least – knock them off balance again.

Combination 7

Leg catch/Block/Roundhouse kick

This combination allows you to catch the attacking leg, before coming back with your own counter. There are a number of good finishes for this, but here we show a low leg roundhouse counter attack. Grabbing the attacker gives you more control as you kick him.

TOP TIP

Remember: once you have caught the kicking leg, pull it into the side of your body, and maintain your hold on it throughout. You can keep the opponent at distance by stretching out his leg.

2▼ As the attcker pushes the kick out, scoop your rear hand under the ankle and catch it. Pull it into the side of your body and stretch out the leg, keeping your opponent at distance from you.

1▲ From the guard position, the attacker lifts his leg up, ready to throw a front leg push kick. Slide your front leg back slightly, to ready yourself for the kick.

3◀ Now the attacker attempts to throw a front hand punch towards your head. Step back and block the punch with your rear hand, still keeping hold of the attacker's leg.

5▲ Now finish by throwing a rear low leg roundhouse to the outside of the attacker's thigh, using your shin. Pull your opponent into you, to drive more power into your kick.

4▶ Lift your rear leg so it is ready to kick, and grab hold of your attacker with your free hand, to help you maintain your balance as you kick.

Combination 8
Clinch/Roundhouse knee/Throw

Here we look at how to work from an attacker's clinch into your own clinch, and then follow up with an attack, to finish with a throw. It is important to move straight in to throw once you have delivered your knee strike, to take advantage of your opponent's vulnerable position.

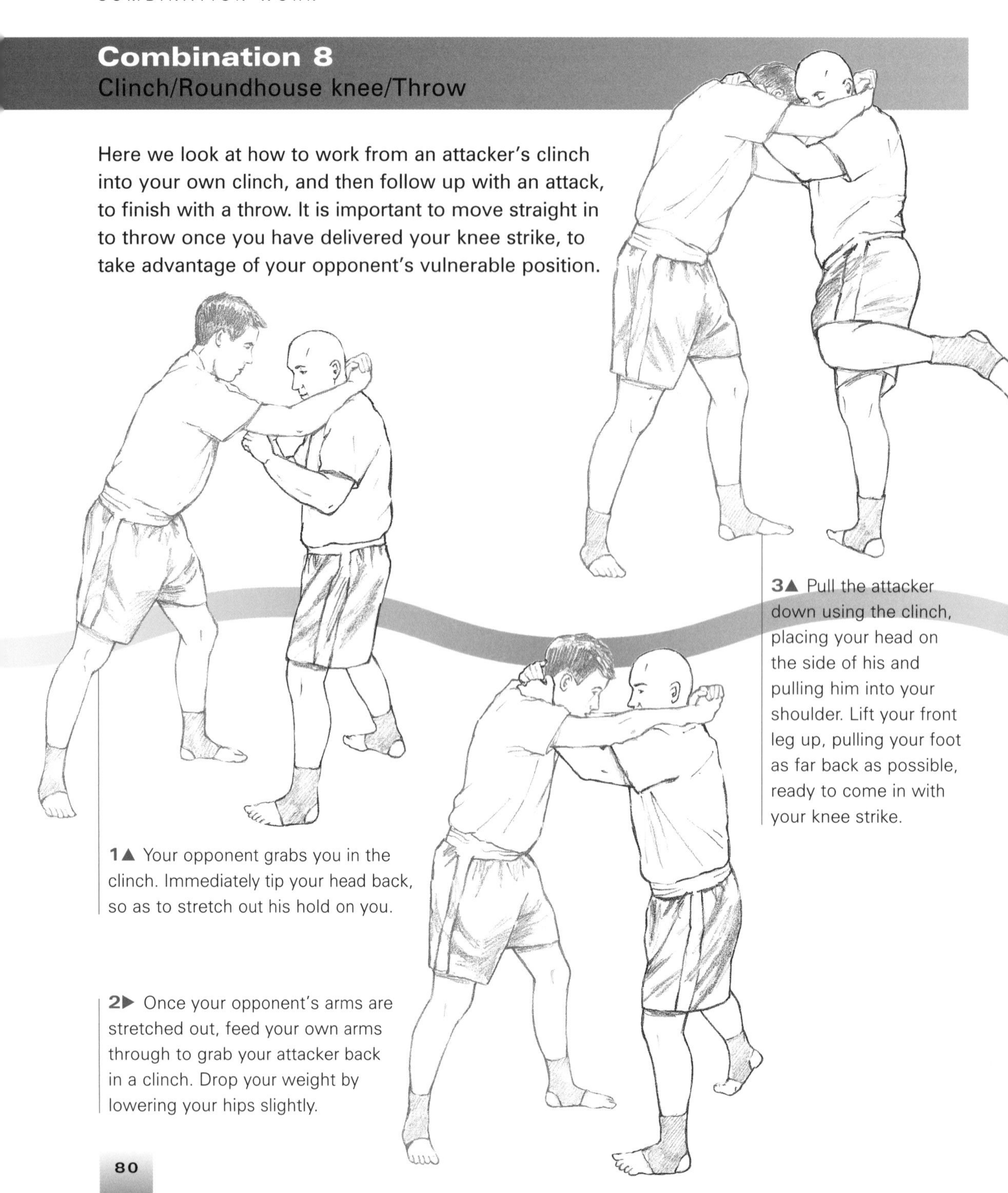

3▲ Pull the attacker down using the clinch, placing your head on the side of his and pulling him into your shoulder. Lift your front leg up, pulling your foot as far back as possible, ready to come in with your knee strike.

1▲ Your opponent grabs you in the clinch. Immediately tip your head back, so as to stretch out his hold on you.

2▶ Once your opponent's arms are stretched out, feed your own arms through to grab your attacker back in a clinch. Drop your weight by lowering your hips slightly.

4◀ After pulling your opponent down, throw a low roundhouse knee strike to the inside of his front leg, knocking him off balance and weakening him.

5▼ Immediately step across your opponent and prepare to throw him. Loosen your clinch, but do not let go.

6▼ Now finish by throwing your opponent away: spin him around as you throw your rear leg backwards and around behind you, to bring him to the floor.

TOP TIP
You must pull your head back once you have been clinched, to weaken your attacker's hold. When preparing to throw him, don't let go, or he will have a chance to escape.

Combination 9
Jab/Cross/Uppercut/Roundhouse elbow

This combination features three punches followed by an elbow strike, and demonstrates how to move in on an attacker when you begin just beyond punching range, to then finish the attack at close range.

TOP TIP
After your jab and cross, slide into your next two strikes to bring you into close range. Rolling your shoulder will give you greater flexibility in your elbow strike.

2▼ Straight after your jab, as you are pulling your arm back, rotate your hips and throw out a cross punch, again to the head/face of your opponent.

1▲ From your position just outside punching range, move in closer to your opponent, and as you move in throw out a jab punch to his head.

3◀ Pull back the cross punch, slide in closer, and now rotate your hips back the other way, throwing a front hand uppercut punch under the chin of your opponent.

4▶ Now finish your attack with an elbow strike, again rotating your hips back the opposite way, rolling your shoulder to strike the side of the face with a roundhouse elbow.

Combination 10
Roundhouse kick/Spinning hook kick

This combination shows a high front roundhouse kick followed by a spinning hook kick. If the roundhouse kick connects correctly, there would normally be no need for the spinning hook, but if the first kick misses the target, this is a good way to follow on immediately with a second attack.

1▲ From a front fighting stance, throw a front leg roundhouse kick towards your opponent's head. He sees this coming, and throws his head back, out of the way of the attack.

2▶ Because you have missed your target, the momentum of your kick carries your leg around, so that you land awkwardly, beyond your normal stance. Your opponent sees this, and moves in.

3◀ As your opponent moves in, continue the rotation of your body (carrying through the momentum of the first 'missed' kick), and swing your opposite leg around, in a spinning hook kick to the head.

TOP TIP

To achieve a good spinning hook kick, continue your spin straight after you miss with the front roundhouse kick, to make your attack one fluid movement. Don't stop and start.

4▲ After striking your target, let the full momentum of the leg swing bring your leg back around, to land in your normal fighting stance. This brings you back to a position where you can continue with further attacks if you wish.

Combination 11
Front kick/Roundhouse kick/Cross

In this combination of two kicks and one punch, both kicks come from the front leg, in your normal fighting stance. The punch only comes into play once you have unbalanced your opponent with your second kick, a low leg roundhouse.

TOP TIP
After each kick, pull straight back to a full guard and stance. Remember: whenever you are looking towards a target area, take care not to signal your intentions to your opponent.

1▲ Beginning in your fighting stance, with your guard held high, throw out a high front leg snap kick, up through the guard of your opponent.

2▶ Bring your kicking leg straight back down to land in front of you, back to your fighting stance, and keep your guard. Take a quick look at your next striking target.

4▼ The kick will have unbalanced your opponent, so take advantage of this to now finish by bringing your kicking leg straight back down in front of you and turning your hips to throw a rear cross punch to your opponent's head.

3▲ After assessing your target area (be careful not to signal your attack to your opponent!), throw a low roundhouse kick – using the shin – to the inside of your opponent's front leg.

Combination 12
Jab/Roundhouse kick/Spinning side kick

In this combination, the jab functions mainly as a decoy, to make your opponent lift his guard higher, giving you the chance to then throw two quick body kicks. Once the roundhouse kick has connected, you can continue to spin around into a side kick, using the momentum gained from the spin to knock your opponent back.

1▼ From your guard, throw out a jab towards your opponent's face. This will cause him to pull his guard higher, opening up the body area to attack.

2▲ As soon as you see this happen, pull your jabbing hand back while simultaneously throwing a front leg roundhouse kick to the body of your opponent. You can use either the shin or the ball of the foot to hit the target area.

3◀ Pull your roundhouse kick back and bring your leg around so that your back is to your opponent. Keep your eyes on the target, looking over your shoulder as soon as you turn your back.

4▼ Quickly turn your head the opposite way, spinning your body as you do this, and throw out a side kick with the opposite leg to the midsection of your opponent. The combined power of the spin and the kick should be enough to topple him off balance.

TOP TIP
Make sure you keep your eyes on your opponent as you turn your back, and remember to thrust in using your hips, to give you more drive in your kick.

Combination 13
Jab/Roundhouse elbow/Jumping rising knee

This combination includes one of the jumping knee techniques of Thai Boxing, which can do a great deal of damage when connected correctly. Don't overlook the jab and the elbow strike at the beginning of the sequence; these are both important in lining up your opponent for your knee strike.

TOP TIP
Depending on which stance you use (left or right), you must place your hands on the opposite shoulder to pull your opponent down. Remember that you can use either the body or the head as a target – depending on your agility!

2▼ When you see the head go back, slide in off your front leg and throw a rear roundhouse elbow strike to the side of your opponent's head.

1▲ Straight from your guard, throw out a front hand jab to your opponent's face. When this connects, it will tip his head back, allowing you to move in with your next strike.

5▶ From your dropped stance, push on your opponent and jump up, striking with a rising knee to either the midsection or the head (both can be used as a target in this attack).

3▲ After delivering the elbow strike, reach over and place both hands just over your opponent's right shoulder (or left shoulder, if done in the opposite stance).

4▶ Now pull your opponent downwards, sinking your weight right down, bending at the knees as you pull, ready to spring back up to attack with your knee strike.

Combination 14
Jab/Cross/Side kick

This combination is a good example of how to come through with a successful attack after your first two attempts have been blocked. Although your punches may fail to reach the intended target, they succeed in forcing your opponent to expose their body area, leaving you the chance to throw out a front leg side kick.

TOP TIP
Don't move in too close with your punches, as you need to have some distance to throw in a good side kick. Make sure you pull your cross punch straight back, while turning sideways on, ready to kick.

1▲ From your guard, throw out a front hand jab towards your opponent's face. They see this coming, and block it with a rear hand parry.

2▼ As your opponent has blocked your jab, now throw out a rear hand cross punch towards his head. Again your punch is blocked, this time with a front hand parry.

3◀ Now pull back your punching arm and turn your body sideways on to your opponent, pulling up your guard and lifting your front leg, chambering ready to execute your kick.

4▶ As your opponent moves in, thrust out a side kick into their body. This will push them backwards, or make them fold at the waist, allowing you to then move in with another attack.

Combination 15
Jab/Cross/Roundhouse kick/Front kick

In this combination you will be attacking with two punches and two kicks, both off the front leg. You will be using the instep part of your foot when executing the roundhouse kick, as you will then be following on with a front kick. To fell your opponent, you would use the shin.

1▲ Begin in your normal fighting stance. Throw out a front hand jab to your opponent's face, connecting and knocking the head back.

2▲ Pull back your jabbing hand and rotate your hips, coming up onto the ball of your rear foot, and now throw out a rear cross punch to the face of your opponent.

3◀ Pull back your punching arm, then throw in a front leg roundhouse kick to the inside of your opponent's leg, using the instep part of your foot to slap against the thigh.

4▼ Now bring the kicking leg back down to land in front of you, not resuming your normal stance but instead coming up onto the ball of your front foot.

5▲ As your opponent moves in after your roundhouse kick, throw out a front leg push kick straight into their midriff, to finish your attacking combination.

TOP TIP

Remember to use the instep part of your foot for the roundhouse kick, as your aim here is to weaken your opponent's stance and maintain the correct distance to follow in with your front kick. Make sure you are up on the ball of your kicking foot, ready to deliver your second kick.

Combination 16
Front kick/Roundhouse knee/Hook/Roundhouse elbow

This combination puts together a kick, a knee strike, a punch and an elbow strike – an attack from each of the weapons of Thai Boxing. All the techniques come together here in one constant attack on your opponent.

TOP TIP
Move into all of your attacks, and rotate your hips straight from the hook punch into the elbow strike, to increase the drive and power in your elbow.

2▼ Walking forward, start moving into your opponent, keeping your guard as you do this.

1▲ After squaring off, move in and throw a front leg push kick into your opponent, knocking him back.

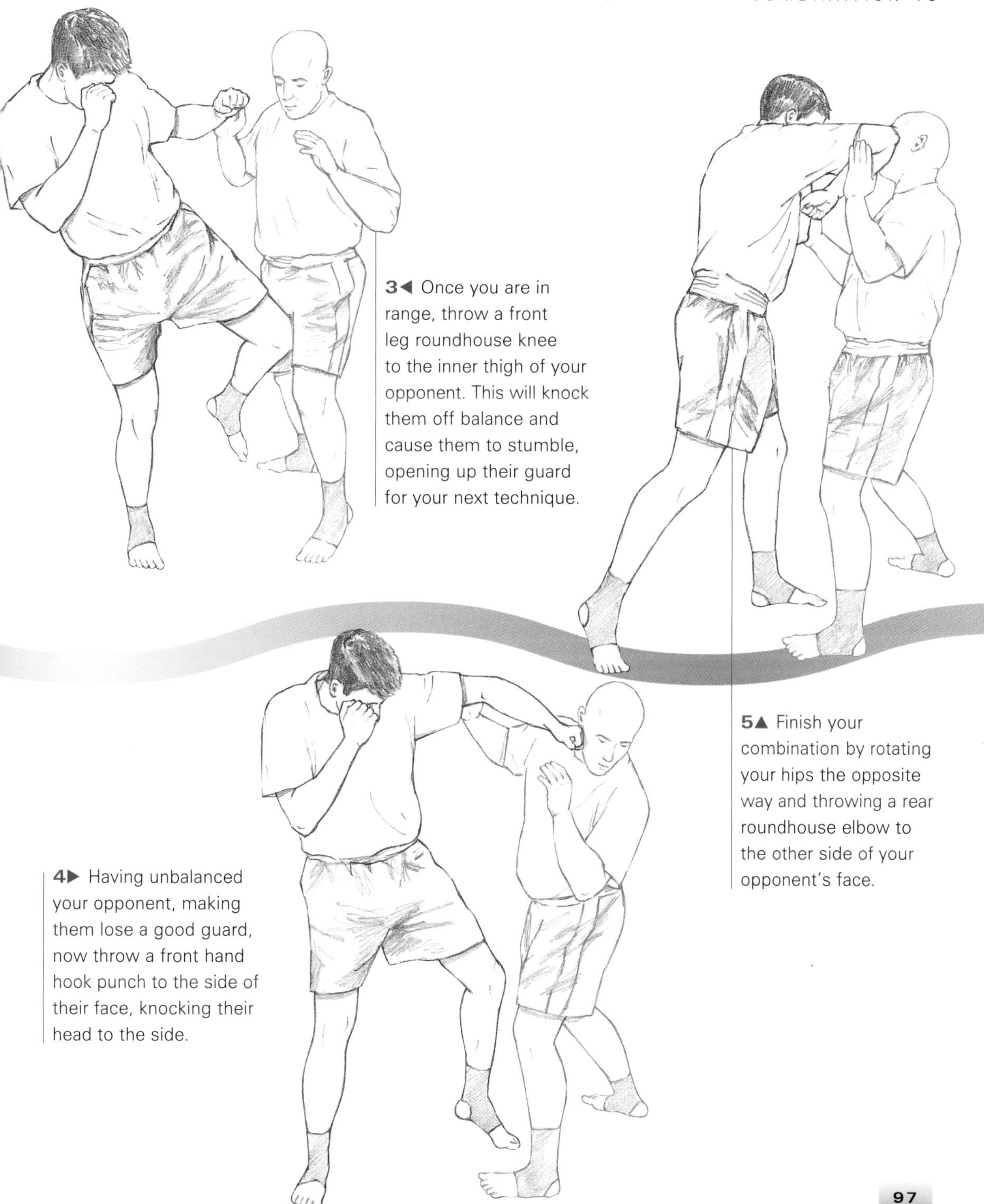

3◀ Once you are in range, throw a front leg roundhouse knee to the inner thigh of your opponent. This will knock them off balance and cause them to stumble, opening up their guard for your next technique.

5▲ Finish your combination by rotating your hips the opposite way and throwing a rear roundhouse elbow to the other side of your opponent's face.

4▶ Having unbalanced your opponent, making them lose a good guard, now throw a front hand hook punch to the side of their face, knocking their head to the side.

SELF-DEFENCE

Punch counter

Thai Boxing techniques can be effectively applied as a means of self-defence. Here we see how to defend against an attacker who comes at you with a rear hand hook-type punch – first to block the attack, then to counter, finally pushing the attacker away so you can make your escape.

TOP TIP
After you have pushed the attacker away, move away from them immediately, for your own safety. Your strikes should have done enough damage.

2▼ Having blocked the punch, place your blocking arm on the attacker's arm, grabbing between the upper arm and shoulder.

1▲ You are attacked by someone who throws a rear hand punch to your face. Stop this by throwing your front arm up into a high forearm block.

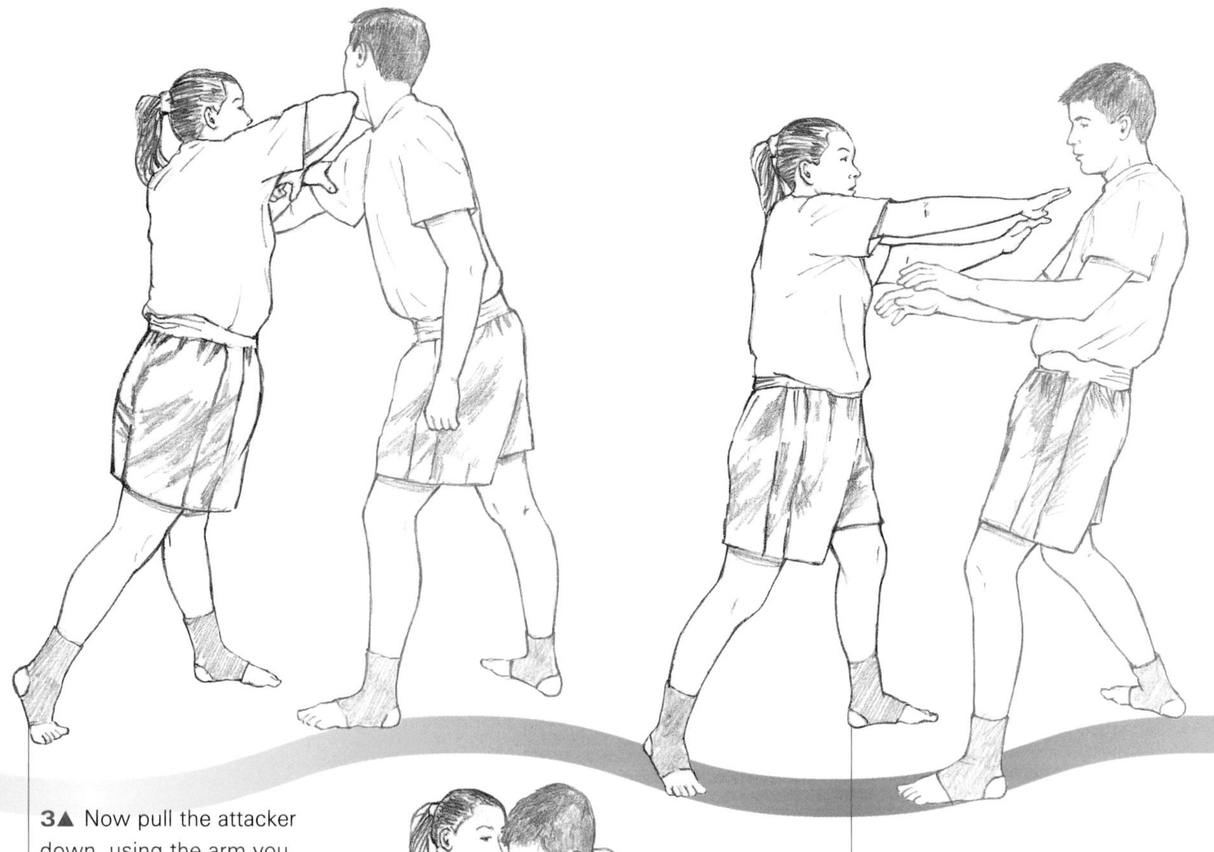

3▲ Now pull the attacker down, using the arm you have grabbed to control him, and throw a rear roundhouse elbow to his head, knocking it sideways.

4▶ Immediately after delivering your elbow strike, place your hand on the attacker's shoulder, and pull him down as you strike with a rising knee to his midsection.

5▲ When you have struck with your knee, place your leg straight back down on the floor. Standing in a strong stance, put both your hands on the shoulders of your attacker, and push him back, to move him away.

Wrist-grab counter

This sequence shows you what to do if someone grabs you by both wrists, first pulling away from the attacker, and then countering back with an elbow strike and low kick to the attacker's shin. The hand-release technique is key: it's important to get this right, or you may find you are unable to release yourself from the attacker's grip.

TOP TIP
Remember to twist the wrist *before* you pull back from the wrist grab. When you kick, if wearing soft footwear, use the ball of the foot; with strong footwear, you can use the tip.

1▲ The attacker grabs you tightly by both wrists, intending not to let you go.

2▲ Step back sharply, placing your right leg behind you. This will cause your attacker to stumble forward, making your release easier.

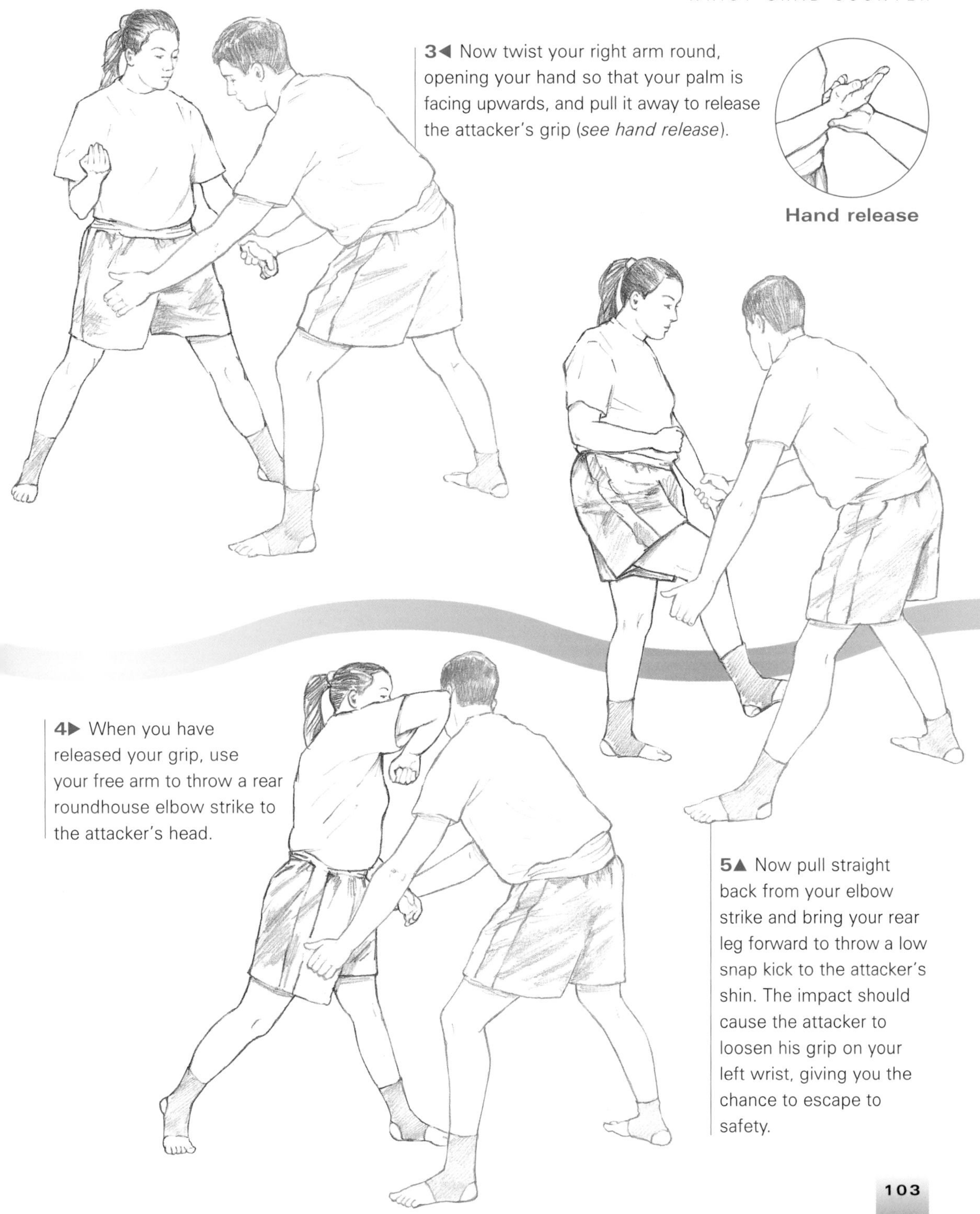

3◀ Now twist your right arm round, opening your hand so that your palm is facing upwards, and pull it away to release the attacker's grip (*see hand release*).

Hand release

4▶ When you have released your grip, use your free arm to throw a rear roundhouse elbow strike to the attacker's head.

5▲ Now pull straight back from your elbow strike and bring your rear leg forward to throw a low snap kick to the attacker's shin. The impact should cause the attacker to loosen his grip on your left wrist, giving you the chance to escape to safety.

Lapel-grab counter

This sequence demonstrates how to defend against an attack from the front, when you are grabbed by your clothing. The clinch hold now comes into play, allowing you to follow up with a knee strike to the groin and finally to get rid of your attacker by throwing him to the ground.

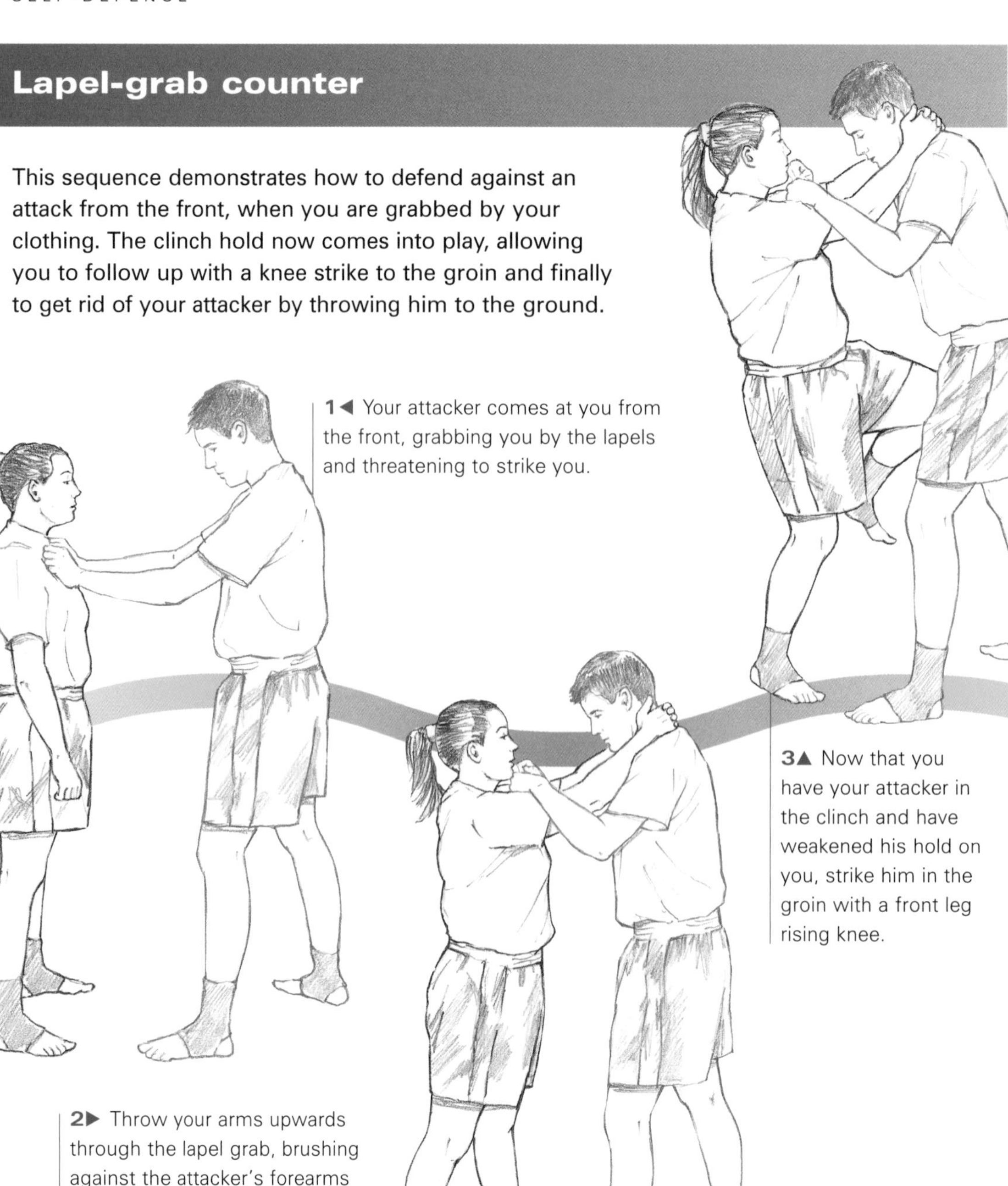

1◀ Your attacker comes at you from the front, grabbing you by the lapels and threatening to strike you.

2▶ Throw your arms upwards through the lapel grab, brushing against the attacker's forearms to weaken his grip, and grab him round the back of the neck, in the clinch hold.

3▲ Now that you have your attacker in the clinch and have weakened his hold on you, strike him in the groin with a front leg rising knee.

4◀ This will weaken the attacker further, and make him release his hold on you. Keep your own clinch hold tight, and begin to throw the attacker around, away from you.

TOP TIP
Remember to brush your arms against the attacker's forearms when feeding them through for the clinch, to weaken the attacker's grip. When you throw your attacker to finish, make sure you lower your weight as you are turning.

5▶ Continue throwing the attacker around using your clinch hold, lowering your weight and dragging the attacker down. When they hit the floor, release your grip, as this will now give you the chance to escape.

Arm-grab counter

If an attacker grabs you by one wrist, you may be able to twist your arm out of the hold, but this still leaves you with the threat of another attack. Instead, you can use the hold to your advantage, to unbalance your attacker, so giving you the opportunity to move in with your own counter attack and escape to safety.

TOP TIP
Use the ball of the foot when you snap kick to the knee; it is a bigger striking area than the tip, and gives you sufficient power to ensure that you fell your attacker. Make sure you come up onto the balls of your feet as you stretch your arm up for the elbow strike, so that you can really drive your elbow down.

1▲ An attacker comes at you from the front and grabs one of your wrists. Prepare to pull your arm backwards.

2▼ Pull your arm back sharply, making the attacker stumble forward and lose his balance. Quickly follow this with a front leg snap kick, using the ball of your foot, to his knee.

3▶ The kick to the knee will fell your attacker, making him expose his back in front of you. Come up onto the balls of your feet, lifting your rear arm right up, ready to move in with your next strike.

4▶ Now drop right down, bending at the knees, with your rear knee underneath you, and deliver a downward elbow strike to the upper back of your attacker. This will drop him completely to the floor, giving you the chance to escape while he is incapacitated.